EDUCATION, POLITICS, AND PUBLIC LIFE

Series Editors:
Henry A. Giroux, McMaster University
Susan Searls Giroux, McMaster University

Within the last three decades, education as a political, moral, and ideological practice has become central to rethinking not only the role of public and higher education, but also the emergence of pedagogical sites outside of the schools—which include but are not limited to the Internet, television, film, magazines, and the media of print culture. Education as both a form of schooling and public pedagogy reaches into every aspect of political, economic, and social life. What is particularly important in this highly interdisciplinary and politically nuanced view of education are a number of issues that now connect learning to social change, the operations of democratic public life, and the formation of critically engaged individual and social agents. At the center of this series will be questions regarding what young people, adults, academics, artists, and cultural workers need to know to be able to live in an inclusive and just democracy and what it would mean to develop institutional capacities to reintroduce politics and public commitment into everyday life. Books in this series aim to play a vital role in rethinking the entire project of the related themes of politics, democratic struggles, and critical education within the global public sphere.

SERIES EDITORS:

HENRY A. GIROUX holds the Global TV Network Chair in English and Cultural Studies at McMaster University in Canada. He is on the editorial and advisory boards of numerous national and international scholarly journals. Professor Giroux was selected as a Kappa Delta Pi Laureate in 1998 and was the recipient of a Getty Research Institute Visiting Scholar Award in 1999. He was the recipient of the Hooker Distinguished Professor Award for 2001. He received an Honorary Doctorate of Letters from Memorial University of Newfoundland in 2005. His most recent books include *Take Back Higher Education* (co-authored with Susan Searls Giroux, 2006); *America on the Edge* (2006); *Beyond the Spectacle of Terrorism* (2006); *Stormy Weather: Katrina and the Politics of Disposability* (2006); *The University in Chains: Confronting the Military-Industrial-Academic Complex* (2007); and *Against the Terror of Neoliberalism: Politics Beyond the Age of Greed* (2008).

SUSAN SEARLS GIROUX is Associate Professor of English and Cultural Studies at McMaster University. Her most recent books include *The Theory Toolbox* (co-authored with Jeff Nealon, 2004) and *Take Back Higher Education* (co-authored with Henry A. Giroux, 2006), and *Between Race and Reason: Violence, Intellectual Responsibility, and the University to*

Come (2010). Professor Giroux is also the Managing Editor of *The Review of Education, Pedagogy, and Cultural Studies.*

Critical Pedagogy in Uncertain Times: Hope and Possibilities
Edited by Sheila L. Macrine

The Gift of Education: Public Education and Venture Philanthropy
Kenneth J. Saltman

Feminist Theory in Pursuit of the Public: Women and the "Re-Privatization" of Labor
Robin Truth Goodman

Hollywood's Exploited: Public Pedagogy, Corporate Movies, and Cultural Crisis
Edited by Benjamin Frymer, Tony Kashani, Anthony J. Nocella, II, and Richard Van Heertum; with a Foreword by Lawrence Grossberg

Education out of Bounds: Reimagining Cultural Studies for a Posthuman Age
Tyson E. Lewis and Richard Kahn

Academic Freedom in the Post-9/11 Era
Edited by Edward J. Carvalho and David B. Downing

Educating Youth for a World beyond Violence
H. Svi Shapiro

Rituals and Student Identity in Education: Ritual Critique for a New Pedagogy
Richard A. Quantz with Terry O'Connor and Peter Magolda

Citizen Youth: Culture, Activism, and Agency in a Neoliberal Era
Jacqueline Kennelly

Conflicts in Curriculum Theory: Challenging Hegemonic Epistemologies
João M. Paraskeva

America According to Colbert: Satire as Public Pedagogy post-9/11
Sophia A. McClennen (forthcoming)

Citizen Youth

Culture, Activism, and Agency in a Neoliberal Era

Jacqueline Kennelly

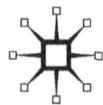

CITIZEN YOUTH
Copyright © Jacqueline Kennelly, 2011.
Softcover reprint of the hardcover 1st edition 2011 978-0-230-10668-0
All rights reserved.

First published in 2011 by
PALGRAVE MACMILLAN®
in the United States—a division of St. Martin's Press LLC,
175 Fifth Avenue, New York, NY 10010.

Where this book is distributed in the UK, Europe and the rest of the world, this is by Palgrave Macmillan, a division of Macmillan Publishers Limited, registered in England, company number 785998, of Houndmills, Basingstoke, Hampshire RG21 6XS.

Palgrave Macmillan is the global academic imprint of the above companies and has companies and representatives throughout the world.

Palgrave® and Macmillan® are registered trademarks in the United States, the United Kingdom, Europe and other countries.

ISBN 978-1-349-29032-1   ISBN 978-0-230-11961-1 (eBook)
DOI 10.1057/9780230119611
Library of Congress Cataloging-in-Publication Data

Kennelly, Jacqueline.
   Citizen youth : culture, activism, and agency in a neoliberal era / Jacqueline Kennelly.
    p. cm.
    1. Urban youth—Political activity—Canada. 2. Social movements—Canada. 3. Subculture—Canada. I. Title.
HQ799.C2K46 2011
303.48'408350971—dc22   2011001490

A catalogue record of the book is available from the British Library.

Design by Newgen Imaging Systems (P) Ltd., Chennai, India.

First edition: July 2011
10 9 8 7 6 5 4 3 2 1

For

*KaiLin Kennelly Duong,
my future Citizen Youth*

Contents

Acknowledgments	ix
Introduction: "Citizen Youth" in the Twenty-first Century	1
1 Understanding Youth Political Engagement: Youth Citizenship as Governance	19
2 Constructing the Good Youth Citizen: A History of the Present	33
3 Good Citizen/Bad Activist: The Cultural Role of the State in Youth Political Participation	47
4 Class Exclusions, Racialized Identities: The Symbolic Economy of Youth Activism	73
5 Becoming Actors: Agency and Youth Activist Subcultures	111
6 Conclusions	133
Appendix: Research Methods	143
Notes	161
References	169
Index	185

Acknowledgments

Any piece of academic or creative work is built upon a foundation of relationships and support, and this one is no exception. I have been fortunate enough to be surrounded, at all stages of development of this work, by friends, family, and colleagues who have given me the resources, feedback, and words of wisdom that have allowed me to proceed. The original dissertation upon which this book is based was nurtured through from inception to completion under the thoughtful and insightful guidance of my doctoral supervisor, Jo-Anne Dillabough, to whom I owe more than she will ever know. Her keen theoretical mind, her deep commitment to truth and justice, and her outstanding mentoring skills permeate the book from start to finish. Mona Gleason and Deirdre Kelly were also essential to the successful completion of that original project, and their feedback and support continue to shine through in this final book version of the work. Kari Dehli, Kathleen Gallagher, and Roger Simon were pivotal in providing me with academic community and research space during the fieldwork period in Toronto. Without you all, this project would never have happened.

More recently, I have benefited tremendously from the institutional support of Diane Reay, my postdoctoral supervisor at the University of Cambridge, and Peter Gose, chair of the Department of Sociology and Anthropology at Carleton University, where I currently work. They each permitted me the space and facilities that allowed me to convert the original dissertation into its final book form. Susan Valentine, Stuart Poyntz, Bernhard Leistle, Jen Pylypa, Justin Paulson, Xiaobei Chen, and Augustine Park all played key roles at various points in the manuscript's development, through feedback on early chapters and the draft prospectus. I owe a big debt of gratitude to Susan Searles Giroux, who first encouraged me to submit my prospectus to Palgrave, and a further debt to her and Henry Giroux for including this book within their series. Deep thanks to my cheerful and indomitable editor at Palgrave, Burke Gerstenschlager, who stood by me and cheered me on from the sidelines during the final few months before the deadline, as circumstances threw barrier after barrier in my path. Likewise to the two editorial assistants with whom I had the pleasure to work, Samantha Hasey and Kaylan Connally, who helped sort through the final nitty-gritty of bringing this project to completion. I owe a huge debt to Karen Tucker, who literally became my left arm in order to complete the manuscript (almost to deadline), and Marlene Brancato and all of the other administrative staff in the Department of Sociology and Anthropology at Carleton University, who worked tirelessly to get me the support I needed when life was getting in the way.

Revised versions of sections of this book have previously appeared or are soon to be published elsewhere as journal articles. These are:

> Kennelly, J. and K. Llewellyn. (In press). Educating for active compliance: Discursive constructions in citizenship education. *Citizenship Studies.*
>
> Kennelly, J. (2009). Learning to protest: youth activist cultural politics in contemporary urban Canada. *Review of Education, Pedagogy, and Cultural Studies.* Volume 31, Issue 4, pp. 293–316.
>
> Kennelly, J. (2009). Good citizen/bad activist: the cultural role of the state in youth activism. *Review of Education, Pedagogy, and Cultural Studies.* Volume 31, Issues 2–3, pp. 127–149.
>
> Kennelly, J. (2009). Youth cultures, activism, and agency: revisiting feminist debates. *Gender and Education.* Volume 21, Issue 3, pp. 259–272.
>
> Kennelly, J. (2011). Policing young people as citizens-in-waiting: legitimacy, spatiality, and governance. *British Journal of Criminology.* Volume 51, pp. 336–354.

I also wish to acknowledge the support of the Social Sciences and Humanities Research Council of Canada (SSHRC), from whom I received a doctoral scholarship and a postdoctoral fellowship, both of which provided the financial backing that permitted this work to reach fruition. Likewise, a Killam predoctoral fellowship was integral to supporting this work, as were research and travel grants provided by the University of British Columbia's Faculties of Graduate Studies and Education.

On a more personal note, I wish to acknowledge my parents, the pillars of endurance who have seen me through all of life's ups and downs: Barbara Kennelly, Lawrence Cornett, and Kenneth Arenson. I am also grateful to my former spouse, Cuc Duong, who was by my side for most of this project. Though our paths are diverging, I am thankful that she remains a part of my life, as coparent and friend.

Finally, my greatest debt of gratitude is owed to the youth participants themselves, those incredibly inspiring, creative, and energetic individuals who generously shared with me their thoughts, their experiences, and their lives. I hope this work proves useful to them and to others like them who are working hard to make the world a better place.

Introduction

"Citizen Youth" in the
Twenty-first Century

On April 21, 2001, the front page of the *Globe and Mail*, a Canadian national daily newspaper, was dominated by a graphic color photograph of a young man with blood streaming down his face, held tightly between two police officers in full riot gear (figure I.1). The byline to the photo read: "A bloodied protester is arrested yesterday after about 5,000 demonstrators clashed with riot police and crashed through the three-meter high fence surrounding the site of the Third Summit of the Americas in Quebec." The image was one of a series depicting the mass mobilizations that took place in Quebec City from April 20 to 22, 2001, to protest the Free Trade Area of the Americas. It was typical both for its focus on the violent aspects of the protests, and for its representation of young people as the sole participants and instigators.

In January of 2006, *Jane*, an American young women's fashion magazine, dedicated a story to youth activism. Other headlines for that issue included an array of salacious topics common to young women's magazines: "The 15 guys you'll date & dump before you're 30;" "Have fun and get fit: party your way to a better butt," and "The big holiday guide to Instant Beauty: Get dewy skin, sex-kitten hair and lips that stay up all night." The headline about young women's activism could be located just below the left breast of Shakira, a young female musician whose presence on the cover was unrelated to the topic. It read: "Activism special: 5 women like you who are changing the world." Inside, the magazine featured young white women who were making their own "sweatshop free" clothes, buying local

Figure I.1 Fortress Quebec is breached.
Source: Copyright of the Canadian Press/Ryan Remiorz, reprinted with permission.

organic food, renting their second homes out for below-market value, and running a biodiesel station.

These are but two representations of youth activism that confront Western young people in the twenty-first century. On the one hand, youth activists are vilified as irrational, violent, and out-of-control, consistent with a long history of recurrent representations of "rowdy youth as animalistic and subhuman" (McRobbie 1994, 206). On the other hand, they are celebrated as sexy, chic, and desirable, making trendy choices consistent with their middle-class values. This book goes to the heart of these paradoxes and contradictions, exploring the dilemmas and cultural dynamics of being young and politically engaged in the twenty-first century. It takes as its starting point those young people enacting their citizenship through contestation of the state: that is, youth activists. Activism and citizenship are not necessarily easy bedfellows, although the former often presumes access to the latter. This seems to be particularly true for those liberal democratic states that have come to rely on their citizens' capacity to be self-regulating in order to maintain social control (Foucault 1991; Rose 1999). The two representations of young activists presented earlier, I suggest, can be understood as the symbolic edges of a container that encapsulate a certain kind of contemporary youth citizenship. The new twenty-first-century "Citizen Youth" needs to know how to do specific forms of activism, while also paradoxically heeding the associated limits of activism, beyond which "good citizens" dare not tread.

One of the central concerns driving this investigation is that the possibility for creating a public sphere of contestation within liberal democracies is being continually and increasingly placated, repressed, and commodified through institutional, cultural, and social factors, and that this is felt most strongly by young people coming of age in the new millennium. I situate this concern within the uneasy sibling relationship that lies at the center of this study: that is, between the youth citizen and the youth activist. The former is associated with specific qualities and characteristics that are desirable to the nation-state (as opposed to the de facto rights and legal obligations implied by the status of citizenship). The latter, on the other hand, exists as an ambivalent near-relation, sometimes seen as part of the constellation of qualities of the good citizen, while at others demonized as an undesirable element undeserving of recognition. This uneasy coexistence, and what it means for young people navigating their own relationship to the nation-state, is at the core of the investigation undertaken here.

The dilemmas and concerns that this dichotomous relationship between the "good citizen" and the "bad activist" raise were captured most eloquently in a recent petition circulated after the anti-G8/G20 protests that occurred in Toronto in June of 2010. Thousands of people were on the streets protesting the meetings of the G8 and G20, during which world leaders were scheduled to discuss global economic issues. Police response to the protests was swift and brutal, and many stories immediately emerged of excessive police violence, through both mainstream media sources and social networking sites. Among the various expressions of outrage after the protests, one came from a group of educators and academics who lamented the lessons that this brutal police response had offered young people expressing their legal right to peaceful protest. The authors of the petition wrote:

> As educators, we charge the federal and Ontario governments, RCMP, OPP and Toronto Police responsible for G20 security for violating the institution of civic education... Our responsibility as educators is to prepare active citizens with a strong concern for democratic institutions and a sense of duty to participate actively in democratic processes. (Taylor 2010)

The outrage of the petition designers, while entirely appropriate, suggests that this treatment of young people as dangerous threats to the state who are in need of containment is somehow unique to the G8/G20 protests. This book documents that this most evidently is not the case. The recent police response to G8/G20 protesters, particularly young people, is merely the logical extension of influences and forces that have been at play for many years. One of the core aims of this book is to trace the genesis and consequences of these root causes, thinking critically about what citizenship roles young people are permitted to express within twenty-first century liberal democratic states, and what cultural and material limits have been imposed on these roles.

Through an ethnographic study of young people (ages thirteen to twenty-nine) working on activist causes linked to globalization, poverty, war, and colonialism across the three largest urban centers in one of the wealthiest nations in the world (Toronto, Montreal, and Vancouver, Canada), this book explores what it means to be a certain kind of youth citizen in the twenty-first century. Although necessarily grounded within the Canadian context, given the location of the ethnographic fieldwork, the findings might be generalized to other national sites, particularly those with similar histories of colonialism, industrialization, immigration, and liberal/neoliberal democracy. It thus charts a story that is both specific and place-based, *and* transferable across locales, where similar dynamics and social contexts have created similar pressures and responses. Drawing on cultural, sociological, feminist, and phenomenological theories of the self, the state, and social relations, the book attempts to clarify some of the dilemmas of the new millennium with respect to youth political engagement and citizenship.

To this end, it asks three broad questions that address the relationship between young people, the state, and citizenship. First, it questions the role played by the history of state claims about the "good and moral citizen": In what ways do these shape both activist cultures and the potential for young people to enact their activism? Second, it considers who is and who is not able to enact such citizenship, seeking to identify those social and cultural forces that legitimize the "good citizen": What might this mean for political action in a democratic public sphere? Finally, it examines how young people both come to and remain engaged in activism, by exploring the largely classed subcultural pressures and modalities of agency available to them: Who feels that they "belong" within youth activist subcultures, and what implications does this carry for social movements more broadly?

Neoliberalism as Context and Culture

The specific moment in which Citizen Youth exists is marked by particular conditions, labeled alternatively (and sometimes interchangeably) as "modernity" (Bauman 2004), "late modernity" (Young 1999), "postmodernity" (Scott-Bauman 2003), or "risk society" (Beck 1999). Young people are often seen to be at the front edge of the shifting conditions of contemporary society, perceived as both the creators and casualties of changing times (Ball et al. 2000; Bynner et al. 1997). These conditions include, but are not limited to, increasing economic stratification, impending threats of environmental devastation, mass global migration, and such supranational threats as "terrorism." Theorists of modernity have identified the parallel subjectivities that have emerged in high modern times as being marked by individualism, alienation, and depoliticized relations to the state (Bauman 2004; Brown 1995). Various studies have noted the ways in which these characteristics have been taken up by young people in industrialized countries around the world, with a variety of consequences (Dillabough & Kennelly 2010; Luttrell, 1996; McLeod & Yates 2006).

Neoliberalism might be understood as the political and ideological response that has come to dominate this "high modern" era. It is a term most commonly used to signify the set of economic, policy, and political practices that incorporate radical efforts to liberalize markets (and thus create "free markets"), generally achieved through economic deregulation, elimination of tariffs, and cuts to social and health services. It also refers to what Wendy Brown (2005) calls a "political rationality" (38) that organizes these policies, and "carries a social analysis that, when deployed as a form of governmentality, reaches from the soul of the citizen-subject to education policy to practices of empire" (39). Like many Western liberal democratic states over the last thirty years, Canada has increasingly embraced neoliberal practices that have resulted in retrenchment policies in everything from housing to education to welfare. Most noticeably arising in the early 1980s under the federal Progressive Conservatives and Brian Mulroney, the intervening decades have seen colossal cuts to social services, increasing liberalization of trade, the privatization of such common resources as energy and water, and anti-union legislation at both provincial and federal levels (Bashevkin 2000; Canadian Labour Congress 2003; Carroll & Jones 2000; Council of Canadians 2001; Dobbin 2003). Alongside these cuts and priority shifts, urban homelessness has risen (Hargrave 1999), and student debt and youth unemployment have increased inexorably (Beauvais et al. 2001; Statistics Canada 2004). Canada is also witnessing an increasingly strained health care system (Public Health Agency of Canada 2002).

The Canadian political and economic context can be understood as part of a larger and highly mobile global structure of "liberalization" operating in the affluent West that has disciplined countries around the world into reducing public services and opening their borders to trade. This disciplining and economic reordering is built upon previous histories of colonialist expansion and exploitation, and serves to reinforce and maintain global power inequalities (Anderson and Cavanaugh 2000; Bello 2000; Chomsky 1999). Within this global milieu, young people are differently advantaged and disadvantaged depending on their particular location in the social structure, whether that be class, ethnicity, geography, or gender, to name a few of the salient contexts. In Canada, as in many globalized countries of the North, the gap is growing between those who can succeed within the "global marketplace" and those who fall through its ever-widening cracks.[1]

Of the three Canadian cities within which this research was carried out, each has experienced retrenchment policies at different points over the last two decades, although each has followed roughly similar paths toward neoliberalism.[2] Toronto, Canada's largest urban center, is located in the province of Ontario, which is the most populous in the country and widely considered to be at the center of national economic activity. Of the three urban centers examined here, Toronto was the earliest to be engulfed in neoliberal policies, when the provincial Progressive Conservatives under Premier Mike Harris first came to power in 1995. Claiming a "Common Sense Revolution," the Harris Conservatives quickly gutted social and health services in the province, instituting widespread retrenchment policies that resulted in substantially heightened social stratification (Keil 2002). Vancouver, in Canada's westernmost province of British Columbia, began its march toward neoliberalism in earnest in 2001, when the provincial Liberals were elected under Premier Gordon Campbell (Kershaw 2004). Following an almost identical trajectory to that carried out by the Conservatives in Ontario, the BC Liberals quickly began to dismantle what had once been one of the strongest social security nets in the country (Fuller 2001). Montreal, located in the predominantly French-speaking province of Quebec, began to experience the pressures of neoliberalism immediately following the 1995 referendum on sovereignty, when Lucien Bouchard became the leader of the provincial Parti Québecois amid promises to reduce taxes and become "fiscally responsible" (Robert 1997). Although relatively shielded from the worst excesses of neoliberalism by a strong tradition of social networks and a history of dissent against English Canada's policy directions (Anonymous 2002), Montreal and the province of Quebec have nonetheless continued along the neoliberal trajectory mapped out within the rest of the country, strengthened by the 2003 election of the provincial Liberal party under Jean Charest (formerly a federal

Progressive Conservative). Each incursion of neoliberalism has been vigorously protested in all three provinces, ranging from Toronto's Metro Days of Action (Conway 2004) to Quebec's province-wide student strike against tuition hikes in 2005 and British Columbia's ongoing mobilizations by unions and social justice organizations against welfare retrenchment, cuts to health care, and homelessness. Despite these public protests and actions, neoliberalism retains substantial power as a governing ideology within each province.

The neoliberal context described here is the spatial and ideological location through which the young activists within this study have both come of age and come to their political activities. As such, it is an important locus of investigation into both their modes of resistance and their sense of themselves (or subjectivities) that they have developed within the Canadian nation-state. One of the arguments that will be developed in the chapters to come is that these forces of neoliberalism are in many ways the antithesis of political engagement, premised as they are upon an ideology of individualized consumerism and meritocracy and the erosion of collective ties. This has implications for the modes and means by which young people both come to activism, and engage in its practices. The book will attempt to demonstrate how the cultural sphere of the Canadian state combines with neoliberal governmentality to undermine activist practices through two main modes: first, by effectively limiting the imagined possibilities of activist engagement via the construction of a particular type of "good and legitimate citizen" and second, by curtailing the means by which activism is carried out, so that it becomes limited to individualized acts of consumption by apparently choosing subjects.

Moral Panics, Social Movements, and Subcultures

I am not alone in my concern about youth political participation. Media articles, government reports, and pundit commentary within liberal democratic states have in recent years focused exhaustively on the "problem" of youth engagement in the polity. Media and popular response are consistent with the "moral panic" thesis developed by Stanley Cohen (1972/2002) in his seminal book on a different set of youth subcultures, the Mods and Rockers. Similar to the "problem" of youth participation in gangs, the contemporary moral panic about youth democratic engagement begins from the premise that youth are fundamentally lacking in a specific set of skills or social attitudes that would otherwise allow them to behave consistently with societal expectations. In the case of youth political engagement, the "lack" resides in their citizenship skills, which, in turn, is supposed to explain dropping voter turnouts among young voters across Western liberal democracies (Institute for Public Policy Research 2006; Pammett & LeDuc 2003). Much of the academic and educational response has thus focused on strategies for remedying this apparent civic deficit (Chamberlin 2003; Criddle et al. 2004; Hébert 1997; Levinson 2003; Osborne 2000; Osler & Starkey 2003). While there have been a range of calls for different forms of citizenship education, from "moral education" (Davies et al. 2005) to "global education" (Osler & Starkey 2003), much of this literature has been marked by a troubling lack of reflection on the historical and contemporary meanings of both youthful citizenship and citizenship education. Some scholars place "youth activism" within a straightforward trajectory of political socialization that will lead the young people to become "better citizens," by integrating them deeply into our social traditions (Yates & Younnis 1999). This conception of youth activism is generally conflated with participation in normative community organizations that are not engaged in practices that challenge state policies. Rather than taking "youth citizenship" to be a desirable political end in any straightforward manner, I focus within this book on how the symbolic elements associated with state desires for youth citizenship function, at least in part, to placate youth activism into acceptable forms of liberal individualism.

There is, on the other hand, a small body of literature that addresses the relationship between youth and citizenship in more critical ways. It is concerned with the way in which calls for youth citizenship often overlook the structured ways in which some young people are able to participate whereas others are systematically excluded (Carroll & Jones 2000; Leighton

2004). It is also concerned with how an apolitical, individualistic conception of citizenship can become inscribed onto young people (Harris 2004; Mitchell 2003), and recognizes how citizenship has come to be conflated with duties and responsibilities, rather than rights and entitlements to protections (Best 2003; France 1998; Hall, Coffey, & Williamson 1999). As Anita Harris (2004) notes, new forms of youth citizenship in the twenty-first century are "constituted around responsibilities rather than rights, managed forms of participation, and consumption" (63). These individualizing forms of citizenship can ultimately serve to obscure, for young people, the possibility of taking the kind of political action that might be necessary to challenge the state when its actions or policies are contrary to public beliefs and values (see also Kennelly & Dillabough 2008).

Another body of literature that might reasonably be thought to be interested in the question of youth political engagement is within the field of study known as "new social movement" theory (or NSM). Given my focus on activism, some might wonder why I have not foregrounded my study within this literature in order to address my research questions. The strength of much of the new social movement literature that I have encountered lies in compelling analyses of the collective phenomenon of social action; it focuses less on the internal, symbolic, and cultural aspects of participation in activist cultures. In other words, social movement theory tends to analyze these phenomena from a *macro* rather than a *micro* level. The focus of social movement theory, whether it be the resource mobilization (RM) theories of the 1970s and 1980s (Tilley 1978, 1985; Zald & McCarthy 1979) or the new social movement theories of the 1980s and beyond (Melucci 1989; Touraine 1981, 1988), have focused on the impact of collective actors organizing around economic, political, or cultural issues (Carroll 1992). Even the most recent iteration within this body of literature, which has begun to make use of the term "contentious politics" in place of "social movements" (Tilley & Tarrow 2007), remains focused on the macro and the global, rather than on the individual actors, their relations to others, and their associated places within the cultural sphere.

Some recent texts do consider elements more closely associated with the concerns of this book. Aminzade et al. (2001) examine the effects of emotions, temporality, and leadership on social movements and other collectivities. Stryker et al. (2000) are concerned with themes of selfhood and identity within social movements, and ask questions about why people join social movements, and why some leave movements sooner than others. Other recent studies examine the movements from which I have drawn my participants, specifically antiglobalization, antipoverty, anticolonialism, and antiwar movements as they have manifested within Western liberal democracies such as Canada. Richard Day (2005) focuses on the most recent manifestations of social movement organizing, including antiglobalization actions such as those in Seattle and Quebec, as well as the emergence of Indymedia Centers, and Canadian activist organizations such as OCAP (the Ontario Coalition Against Poverty) and NOII (No One Is Illegal). Kevin McDonald (2006) and Amory Starr (2001) likewise speak to and about the larger movements with which many of my participants identify. David Graeber (2009) has written a detailed ethnography documenting many of the actions and movements with which my participants were also involved. While broadly related, theme-wise, to the concerns of this book, these texts remain committed to epistemological approaches that draw upon quite different theoretical traditions than the ones I am using here—that is, they are not framing their studies within a cultural sociological and governmentality framework and they have not explored the topic from the vantage point of state influences on the public sphere (e.g., in the form of citizenship education). Nor are they seeking to understand the symbolic dimensions of youth activism or its forms of classification (see Bourdieu 1984).

In essence, the reason that social movement theory is of less relevance to my work than might be thought of a book about "youth activism" is that ultimately I am not trying to describe or locate a phenomenon called a "social movement." Rather, I am concerned with the subcultural manifestation of a specific identity called "activist" taken up by young people in response to various cultural, social, and political contexts in which they find themselves. While concerned with questions of social change and justice, this project is ultimately focused more on the cultural realm, and what this means for who is able to enact their citizenship through participation in youth activist subcultures, and who, on the other hand, is excluded. In other words, the research turns upon profoundly sociological and cultural questions that stand outside the boundaries of what is defined as, or constitutes, a social movement.

Finally, a note on the term "subculture." My use of the term is indebted to the substantial influence of the now-defunct Birmingham Centre for Contemporary Cultural Studies, which produced some of the most influential texts on youth cultures in the twentieth century (e.g., Cohen 1997; Hebdige 1979; McRobbie 1991; Willis 1977). Unfortunately, this body of work had little to say about youth activism. What scant mention that is made either dismisses youth activists as middle-class hippies trying to escape dreary lives (Clarke, Hall, Jefferson, & Roberts 1976), or mentions their actions only in passing as part of a larger and more coherent social movement (Cohen 1997; for an overview discussion of the subcultural literature in relation to youth resistance, see Harris 2008). Nonetheless, their approach to youth cultures is a necessary departure from previous and subsequent youth studies that focused on youth "deviance" or, more recently, "youth transitions" (for a detailed overview of the field, see Dillabough & Kennelly 2010). Strongly influenced by the work of Pierre Bourdieu, the Birmingham CCCS understand the development of youth subcultures as a creative response that emerges within specific socioeconomic contexts, with their own internal logic and coherence. Following Clarke et al. (1976), I understand "culture" to refer to the ways in which "groups 'handle' the raw material of their social and material existence...A culture includes the 'maps of meaning' which make things intelligible to its members" (10). According to this approach, youth subcultures are "focused around certain activities, values, certain uses of material artifacts, territorial spaces etc which significantly differentiate them from the wider culture" (14). In other words, subcultures exist *in relation to* the wider culture, while simultaneously carving out alternative "maps of meaning" from which they can make the larger social realities intelligible to themselves.

The language of "subcultures" is not without contestation, generating heated debates over the forty years since its emergence as a concept. For example, the question of what constitutes a "subculture," and whether it can be constructively used in considering young people's social affiliations, has been a particularly contentious issue. Some theorists have suggested that terms such as youth "lifestyle" or "neo-tribe" might better capture the fluid nature of youth cultural affiliations (Bennett & Kahn-Harris 2004). There is concern that the notion of "subculture" tends to reify youth cultural affiliations, painting them as more cohesive and internally consistent than they actually are. Peter J. Martin (2004) offers one resolution to this dilemma, pointing out that the notion of subcultures (and other collective groupings) is "useful not as definitions of identifiable groups but rather as *symbolic representations* of fluid, sometimes even amorphous, sets of social relations" (26; emphasis in the original). He suggests that the amorphous and fluid nature of subcultures does not negate their theoretical utility for at least two reasons: first, that "the designation of certain [youth] 'groups'—especially if these are portrayed as being threatening or harmful—is a frequent and often consequential tactic of the mass media" (33), and second, "the identification of such groups may be an important, if more diffuse, way in which individuals can experience a sense of inclusion or exclusion, and a corresponding sense of identity" (ibid.). We can see the former consequence of popular perceptions of youth activist subcultures emerging in media depictions of rampaging youth being restrained by armored police (see figure I.1). The latter utility of subcultures is one that I will explore throughout the book, via the ethnography with activist youth who do, to a certain extent, seek each other out in order to experience a "sense of inclusion" and a "corresponding sense of identity," and who likewise experience being excluded from the subcultural group.

In particular, I retain my use of the term in recognition that it is the closest approximation to what was often identified by participants themselves as a "culture," a "subculture," or, sometimes and in half-jest, a "cult." That is, as loose and flexible as the boundaries might be, nonetheless participants seemed to be able to identify and describe something that I am calling a "youth activist subculture"—whether it was through their own sense of inclusion or exclusion, or by being able to describe the unspoken associated rules. Thus, I am using the term "activist subcultures" as a sort of shorthand, to sum up a diverse but nonetheless recognizable group. While this necessarily imprecise term somewhat problematically incorporates subgroups—such as student activists and community-based activists—that may feel antagonistic toward each other (while often simultaneously sharing members), nonetheless there is a certain shared culture that came out across my field work, enough to justify (for me, at least), the continuing use of "activist subcultures" to describe this range of actors.

Overview of Chapters

This book began with two media depictions that, taken together, provide a symbolic representation of some of the dilemmas and contradictions that inform the questions driving the chapters that follow. On the one hand, we witness the figure of the young activist as troublemaker and hooligan, disrupting the apparently legitimate practices of the state. On the other, we see the young activist as desirable, stylish, and chic, complying with middle-class codes of accomplishment and consumption, and mobilizing the fashionable aspects of activist scripts through acts of charity that do little to challenge state inequalities. One response to these disparate representations is to see them as *not*, in fact, contradictory, but rather as representing the symbolic accommodation of activism into liberal democratic codes that allow it to be placated and, when necessary, policed into acceptable forms of youth citizenship. Through the lens of governmentality theories and cultural sociology, alongside the tools of ethnography, this book will attempt to account for the current configurations of this context as it is expressed by youth activists, as well as trace, where possible, the cultural effects of both the historical and contemporary "good citizen" on Canadian youth activist subcultures.

Ultimately, the core arguments that I make in this book are: (i) the construction of the "good (youth) citizen," as a historical effect and a contemporary cultural symbol, plays a regulating role within youth activist subcultures, emerging as a *structure of feeling* (Williams 1977) that shapes young people's responses to each other, to the state, and to the cultural *field* (Bourdieu 1997) of activism; (ii) in partial response to this historical and cultural context, contemporary youth subcultural activism has come to be grounded in exclusionary forms of social conflict, specifically along lines of "race," gender, and class, although these elements tend to be masked both within and outside of youth activist subcultures; and (iii) the cultural *field* of youth activism functions such that young people often come to activism through relational, interactional processes that, while embedded within the constraining features of a regulated social world, also open up possibilities for emergent practices and strengthened political opposition to unjust state structures.

To explore these claims, the book is divided into five chapters. In chapter one, I develop an extended theoretical analysis of governmentality and its intersection with youth citizenship. Specifically, I examine the notion of youth citizenship as governance, considered in light of the political and cultural effects of neoliberalism in Canada and elsewhere. There are specific connections and contradictions inherent to the concepts of "youth" and "citizenship," where each in some way mirrors the other and reinforces its discursive role within the nation-state. The unique contribution offered here is to understand this relationship not as accidental but as inherent to the very governance role played by the idea of the "good young citizen." This chapter is intended as the wider theoretical frame within which to understand the cultural role played by the nation-state at the micro-sociological level of young people's everyday experiences of activism.

Chapter two expands this approach to incorporate a more detailed process of historicization, deeply consonant with the theoretical and methodological approach that informs this study. Broadly speaking, I see the theory and methodology as joined through a phenomenological and hermeneutic lens that incorporates a Ricoeurian "detour"—a process by which to highlight the connections and symbolic mediations between apparently unrelated elements of the social world in order to reveal new insights into the genesis of contemporary social problems. Chapter two provides both an overview of this approach, as well as constituting the historical "detour" through the realm of legitimized youth citizenship as represented by the state-sanctioned development of citizenship education.

In chapter three, we encounter for the first time the narratives of the young activists who participated in this research. Drawing on cultural theories of the individual and the state, as well as feminist theories about gender roles and political participation, this chapter explores how state histories, morality claims, and neoliberal cultural norms intersect to create specific opportunities and limits for youth activist practices. Specifically, the chapter traces the complex relationship young activists have to school-sanctioned forms of citizenship as activism, often forged as a relation of voluntarism within community-based projects. It looks at the manifestation of neoliberal cultural pressures within the personal expressed emotions of the young activists, and how these are intensified as they intersect with gender regimes. Finally, it considers how the tension between the "good citizen" and the "bad activist" manifests beyond the realm of schooling through, for example, encounters with police.

In chapter four, I turn to a specific investigation of the *symbolic economies* of youth activist cultures. Within this chapter, I show precisely how youth activist subcultures are sometimes implicated in, and sometimes inadvertently reproduce, the very forms of exclusion they are seeking on a conscious level to contest. Drawing on Bourdieu's concepts of *habitus, field,* and *authorized language*, I examine the embeddedness of youth activist practices in larger political and cultural frames, looking critically at the question of *who* has the capacity to participate in activist politics, and who, on the other hand, does not have access to the particular cultural resources necessary to become "the activist." I then move forward to connect this cultural analysis to the historical and contemporary influences of dominant constructions of the "good citizen," in order to investigate as far as possible the quite new premises and boundaries framing cultural elements of youth activist cultures within a high modern, neoliberal state. I am particularly interested in exploring here the ways in which youth activism exists as a specific cultural phenomenon within the contemporary moment, seeing it as one response to the increasingly pervasive pressure on young Canadians to become a particular kind of "good citizen," and how, as such, it ultimately carries with it both emancipatory and restrictive potentials.

Finally, in keeping with the potential and associated possibilities for new concepts of freedom (see Brown 2005; Rose 1999) and political engagement, in chapter five I move forward to consider the ways in which young people embrace diverse modalities of action, even in the face of both overwhelming cultural constraints and the raced, gendered, and classed limits of activist cultures. Building on the work of feminist theorists and sociologists concerned with questions of *agency*, I argue for a revised understanding of the potential for political agency among young people, one that accounts for the material and symbolic constraints to youth citizenship as well as the fluidity inherent to a social space constituted in part through interpersonal relationships. Turning in particular to a notion of a *relational modality of agency*, I offer an empirical and theoretical account of how young people can come to alternative forms of political engagement that challenge wider injustices, and are able to continue the important work of advocating for progressive social change. I close the book with a concluding chapter, chapter six, which offers reflections on the implications of my analysis for youth engagement, education, and social movements themselves.

1

Understanding Youth Political Engagement: Youth Citizenship as Governance

> In order to understand what power relations are about, perhaps we should investigate the forms of resistance and attempts made to dissociate these relations.
> —Foucault 1994b, 329

The governance role played by the concept of youth citizenship is one that is disguised on many levels by common linguistic use and hidden assumptions associated with both the concept of "youth" and that of "citizen." One might catch glimpses of the underlying meanings through examples gleaned from the real world of political interactions, particularly when young people attempt to take up an activist role that challenges the state. Susie Weller (2007) recounts the experiences of young people who participated in British antiwar demonstrations in 2003; rather than being praised for their involvement, they were instead "patronized and punished" (21). One young woman was banished from her school for a month as a result of her participation in the marches, and protested her exclusion to the level of the High Court: "Despite winning her case the judge deemed her to be a 'very silly girl'" (ibid.). In an American ethnography of youth activism, Hava Gordon (2010) observes "the extent to which youth are ultimately conceptualized by all adult parties as citizens-in-the-making, not developed enough as political beings to be held fully accountable for their collective action" (94). Likewise, youth in my study often found themselves patronized and dismissed for their activism (if not coerced by police or courts), particularly if it fell outside of the laudable elements of the "good youth citizen" (i.e., those engaged in community work for the purposes of self-fulfillment and resumé enhancement).

How best to make sense of the experiences of these young activists? The aim of this chapter will be to argue that rather than trying to untangle the dilemmas and contradictions of "youth citizenship," perhaps it makes more sense to comprehend youth citizenship as another factor in what Wendy Brown (2006) has identified as "part of a more general depoliticization of citizenship and power and retreat from political life itself" (89). In other words, what if we understand "youth citizenship" and its curricular equivalent of citizenship education as a form of governance designed not to enhance youth political participation but, in fact, to shore up state credibility and undermine challenges to its legitimacy?

This chapter focuses centrally on the role of the state in constituting, defining, and elucidating the permissible extent to which young people may engage in political activity. It does so through a Foucauldian analysis that recognizes that the state functions as more than a simple sovereign ruler exerting power through the monopoly of violence (Brown 2006). Rather than taking "state" here to mean the somehow direct interventions of those elites who come to power through electoral or designated processes, I understand the state as also "ineffaceably engraved in all of us in the form of the state-sanctioned mental categories acquired via schooling [and elsewhere] through which we cognitively construct the social world" (Wacquant 2005b, 17). The means by which such "state-sanctioned mental categories" are culturally expressed, through, for example, the norms, assumptions, and rules of activist subcultures, will be the subject of the second half of the book. The goal of this chapter, and the one that follows, is to articulate the backdrop against which these subcultures must act; in other words, to elucidate the "common culture" (Willis 1990) that these subcultures are responding to, not through their conscious political actions but through their subcultural symbols such as attire, language, and insider knowledge.

This chapter unfolds as follows: I begin with an overview of the concept of "state" that informs this study, based strongly within governmentality theory as elucidated by Foucault and developed by subsequent scholars. I then turn to the peculiar relationship that exists between "citizenship" and "youth," and the implications of this for youth action within the public sphere. I conclude with some thoughts on how these interconnected concepts influence each other in order to create both individualized *structures of feeling* and a wider cultural space that heavily curtails youth political participation within a public sphere of state contestation.

Governmentality, Neoliberalism, and Youth Political Participation

In reflecting on the emergence of what have since come to be known as "new social movements" (largely women's, peace, and student movements of the 1960s and 1970s), Michel Foucault (1994b) suggests that "these struggles are not for or against the 'individual'; rather, they are struggles against the 'government of individualization'" (330). He goes on:

> I don't think that we should consider the 'modern state' as an entity that was developed above individuals, ignoring what they are and even their very existence, but, on the contrary, as a very sophisticated structure in which individuals can be integrated, under one condition: that this individuality would be shaped in a new form, and submitted to a set of very specific patterns. (334)

Under Foucault's unique treatment (1991), the "state"—as a recognizable entity tightly associated with parliament, legal structures, and military—recedes from view, to be replaced by a more dilute and yet nonetheless pervasive system of "government": "Maybe, after all, the state is no more than a composite reality and a mythicized abstraction, whose importance is a lot more limited than many of us think" (103). Recognizing what Foucault calls the essential *governmentalization* of the state means that the state survives, in large part, thanks to processes that are "at once internal and external to the state" (221).

Foucault (1994b) suggests that when the state became primarily a process of government over populations, as opposed to a focus on the protection of territory or the administration of legal systems, it became the means by which "the conduct of individuals or of groups might be directed" (341):

> It covered not only the legitimately constituted forms of political or economic subjection but also modes of action, more or less considered and calculated, that were destined to act upon the possibilities of action of other people. To govern, in this sense, is to structure the possible field of action of others. (Ibid.)

In other words, the state, as used in the Foucauldian tradition within which governmentality studies is situated, must be understood as a process of government that extends beyond the boundaries of directly traceable policy directives or legal decisions (although it is those things also). Rather than seeing any single body—such as the state—as uniquely responsible for governing the conduct of individuals, the governmentality perspective "recognizes that a whole variety of authorities govern in different sites, in relation to different objectives" (Rose et al. 2006, 85). Such governance results in constraints and possibilities emerging for the "field of action" of individuals within the state—in other words, what options become thinkable are shaped in particular ways for specific subjects within the state, in such a way as to ensure the ongoing legitimacy and ultimate survival of the state itself.

Nikolas Rose has expanded upon Foucault's concept of governmentality in an effort to describe the contemporary development of "neoliberal subjectivities." Following Foucault, Rose (1992, 1993, 1999) argues that the advanced forms of liberalism that constitute the nature of the modern nation-state have emerged alongside a particular set of dilemmas about governing its citizens. Rather than resorting to previous forms of overt domination, the modern liberal state developed an apparatus of governance that operates through the "regulated choices of individual citizens" (Rose 1993, 285). It does so by seeking to detach the systems of authority from political rule and instead locating them "within a market governed by the rationalities of competition, accountability, and consumer demand" (ibid.). Thus the human subject is expected to become *self-governing* in ways that uphold, legitimize, and perpetuate the actions of the state. In particular, the liberal state depends on devices, including schooling, prisons, and the family, to "create individuals who do not need to be governed by others, but will govern themselves, master themselves, care for themselves" (289). What is unique about the governmentality perspective is that it does not presuppose a reduction in individual freedom, or suggest that individuals are overtly or ideologically coerced through state apparatuses into performing particular identities; rather, the key to a governmentality perspective is to recognize that individual subjects would "produce the ends of government by fulfilling themselves rather than being merely obedient, and...would be obliged to be free in specific ways" (Rose et al. 2006, 89).

Neoliberalism, as a form of intensified advanced liberalism, Rose argues, has developed particularly powerful forms of governmentality that build upon and extend prior incarnations of liberal governmentality. In relation to the production of particular forms of citizenship, neoliberalism has been successful in integrating at every level of society a concept of the citizen as a "highly individualized consumer-citizen" (Bondi 2005, 499). As Liz Bondi argues, such a form of subjectivity does not necessarily orient all people toward "narcissistic gratification of individual desires via market opportunities" (ibid.); instead, and in a seeming paradox, it can act to support particular forms of political activism, "because activism depends, at least to some extent, on belief in the forms of subjectivity that enable people to make choices about their lives" (ibid.). Such activism is necessarily limited within the context of a neoliberal state, however, as neoliberalism and its associated focus on meritocratic individualism "reduces political citizenship to an unprecedented degree of political passivity and complacency" (Brown 2005, 43). As Wendy Brown notes, "a fully realized neoliberal citizenry would be the opposite of public-minded; indeed, it would barely exist as a public. The body politic ceases to be a body but is rather a group of individual entrepreneurs and consumers" (ibid.). The implications of this narrowing of political citizenship are immediately apparent: if individuals are expected to interact with one another and the state only through their capacity to consume or by an endless focus on self-perfection, the margins of possibility for a collective, communicative, and plural public sphere are substantially narrowed.

Beyond the broadly cultural effects captured by the term "neoliberal subjectivity," neoliberalism as political ideology also has directly material implications for political participation, for youth and adults alike. Daiva Stasiulis (2002) notes that "opportunities for meaningful democratic participation in Canadian public institutions—including governments, schools, and universities—have notably declined with neoliberal governance" (527). This shift is directly related to the neoliberal focus on deficit reduction and "efficiency" as the priority in social welfare expenditure decisions, leading in some cases to the appointment of nonelected representatives to take over from democratically elected bodies.[1] Hava Gordon (2010) likewise notes that "perhaps the overarching phenomenon that not only structures youth but also fostered systems of domination and subordination at the turn of the millennium is the ascendancy of neoliberal ideology" (32). Gordon identifies cuts to public schooling, the corporatization of education, and punitive zero tolerance policies as having real and detrimental effects on student opportunities to become politically engaged. The neoliberal context, while constitutive of widespread social change across dimensions such as class, "race," and gender, also differentially impacts individuals who are already marginalized: "there is...a clear link between being raised in poverty and children's capacity to participate in the decision-making of institutions" (Stasiulis 2002, 518). It is thus significant, and perhaps not surprising, that the findings of this study suggest that it is white, middle-class youth who are still most easily able to access modalities of political engagement through youth activist subcultures (more on this in chapter four).

Youth Citizenship and the Genealogy of Dependency

Wendy Brown (2006) both expands upon and critiques Foucault's theory of governmentality, noting that the state cannot be dispersed to quite the extent that Foucault suggests. She believes that governmentality in fact "shores up the legitimacy of the state and in so doing shores up and expands state power" (82). Specifically, she considers the governmental role that discourses of "tolerance" play in modern (neo)liberal democratic states, suggesting that such discourses act

> as an order of policy discourse that is largely nonlegal without being extralegal, as a state speech act that is only occasionally an enforceable rule... [it is] a discourse that peregrinates between state, civil society, and citizens, that produces and organizes subjects, and that is used by subjects to govern themselves. (79)

She argues that the concept of "tolerance" has come to inculcate all levels of discourse, from policy talk to school-based curricula to celebrity interventions. In doing so, the very term has been rendered opaque, making meaningless any critical dialogue about what tolerance means and what it leaves out. That is, "tolerance" has become a new form of governmentalized morality, where individual subjects are expected to behave in particular ways and espouse particular views, while leaving in place state structures that are actually at the root of social inequalities.

Following Brown, I am suggesting here that discourses of "youth citizenship," and the desirable qualities that are attached to this status—which is not about legal belonging within a state but rather about identity and characteristics seen as valuable by the state—function as a form of governmentality designed simultaneously to shore up state power and disperse potential threats to that power. Just as Brown notes the manner in which "tolerance" both "produces and organizes subjects" and "is used by subjects to govern themselves," so I am arguing that "youth citizenship" has come to achieve each of these ends. What is important here is to "examine how the universalistic criteria of democratic citizenship variously regulate different categories of subjects [and]...these subjects' location within the nation-state and within the global economy" (Ong 1996, 737). In this case, the "universalistic criteria" associated with youth citizenship—which can be traced through a close investigation of the history and present of citizenship education—is, and always has been, a means to placate youth contestation of the state. Exactly how this has come to be will be traced in much greater detail in the next chapter. For the sake of this chapter, I turn now to a closer investigation of the submerged and paradoxical associations attached to the concept of "youth citizenship," in order to further trace the governmental role played by this seemingly innocuous turn of phrase.

The advent of neoliberalism, as both context and culture, has had specific effects on the constitution of youth citizenship, which can be seen with particular clarity through vociferous and multiplying claims about the importance of new forms of citizenship education. Katharyne Mitchell (2003) has cogently analyzed the implications of the neoliberal context for youth citizenship and citizenship education. She points out that "in this neoliberal vision of education, educating a child to be a good citizen is...about attainment of the 'complex skills' necessary for individual success in the global economy" (399). Likewise, in a study of citizenship education in Finland and Britain, Gordon et al. (2000) note the influence of neoliberalism on educational policy, which "contains strong arguments supporting choice, competition and autonomy, and has brought the 'market' into education" (188). Such neoliberal effects occur alongside another ideological position, one that in fact strengthens and reinforces some of the tenets of neoliberalism: that is, citizenship education as training not for *citizens*, but for *citizens-in-the-making*, as people who are inherently "in need of training in the ways of citizenship" (Weller 2007, 30). Young people are positioned in this manner because of the Western construction of children and youth as *dependent*; and dependence, as a quality, is not viewed generously within the context of a neoliberal state.

Within Western states, childhood and youth are constituted in opposition to adulthood, which is semantically and metaphorically associated with independence. Citizenship within liberal democratic traditions is intricately related to the notion of autonomy; this means that the relationship between young people and the idea of "citizenship" is invariably complex and unclear (Bynner 1997; France 1998; Frazer & Emler 1997). In Western liberal democracies, the age at which young people leave school or their parents' home to be independently employed is increasingly extended, thus deferring full citizenship to later points in young peoples' lives (Bynner 1997).[2] The discourse of exclusion of young people on the basis of their dependence emerged fairly recently, arising after World War II in Western liberal democracies such as Canada. Michael Gauvreau (2003) notes:

> [T]hroughout the 1940s, Canadian attitudes and policies on the subject of youth were premised...upon establishing a firm equation between productive work and citizenship. In this dynamic, "adolescents" were defined economically, psychologically, and politically as immature "dependents" whose lack of training and work opportunities rendered them as, at best, unfit for civic life in a democracy and as, at worst, volatile "masses" to be preyed upon by unscrupulous demagogues or potential dictators. (202)

Phillip Mizen (2002) points to the ways in which this continues to hold true today, in a manner that is perhaps even further entrenched. He suggests that the contemporary relationship between young people and the state is "not best understood in terms of a process (or processes) of transition to adult life" (6). Rather, he argues, "youth's continuing significance to the development of capitalist social relations derives from the importance of age to the political management of social relations and to the changing form of the capitalist state" (6). Thus the very notion of an independent, autonomous, rational citizen can be understood to have been partially constructed in relation to its opposite: the dependent, immature, and irrational adolescent.

Nancy Fraser and Linda Gordon (1994) trace the genealogy of the term "dependency," in an attempt to "defamiliarize taken-for-granted beliefs in order to render them susceptible to critique and to illuminate present-day conflicts" (311). In the context of political constructions of "welfare dependency" within the United States in the early 1990s, they argue that dependency is an ideological term that "carries strong emotive and visual associations and a powerful pejorative charge" (ibid.). They describe the image evoked by the term *welfare dependency* as being that of a "young, unmarried black woman (perhaps even a teenager) of uncontrolled sexuality" (ibid.). Interestingly, although Fraser and Gordon highlight the gendered and racialized aspects of this image, they do not incorporate into their analysis the ways in which that third category of "youth" is implicated in common discourses of dependency. Nonetheless, their assessment reveals important implications for youth citizenship, particularly within a neoliberal context.

Prior to the rise of the liberal state, dependency was considered a normal state of being, conceived as a social relation rather than an individual trait. "Thus," Fraser and Gordon note, "it did not carry any moral opprobrium" (313). It did, however, invoke status inferiority, suggesting that one was part of a unit headed by someone else with legal standing. "In a world of status hierarchies dominated by great landowners and their retainers, all members of a household other than its 'head' were dependents, as were free or servile peasants on an estate" (ibid.). They note that the term did not precisely mean *unfree*, but that it did imply a social order in which subjection, not citizenship, was the norm. "*Independence*," they note, "connoted unusual privilege and superiority, as in freedom from labour" (ibid; emphasis in the original). They continue: "Thus, throughout most of the European development of representative government, independence in the sense of property ownership was a prerequisite for political rights. *When dependents began to claim rights and liberty, they perforce became revolutionaries*" (ibid.; emphasis mine). I have highlighted the last statement in this quotation as it bears particular relevance to the construction of youth activists. If young people continue to be "dependents," at a time when independence is understood to be the norm, any attempts to claim their own rights, or to speak out on behalf of the rights of others, will cause them to "perforce become revolutionaries." Thus we can see why the construction of youth as inherently lacking in autonomy, independence, and *citizenship* creates a particular relationship between youth activists and the state. When perceived as inherently dependent and lacking in autonomy, any acts that might be conceived of as those of a full-fledged citizen (such as participating in a protest march, for instance) become suspect. At the least, such actions are seen as irresponsibly precocious; at worst, as the actions of an unaccountable and out-of-control individual unable to recognize or respect consequences.

The postindustrial framing of dependency marked a dramatic shift, prefiguring the particular forms of subjectivity permissible within the liberal and neoliberal state. Specifically, all forms of dependency become "avoidable and [thus] blameworthy" (323). One implication of this trajectory has been an increase in individualization: "With capitalist economic dependency already abolished by definition, and with legal and political dependency now abolished by law, postindustrial society appears to some conservatives and liberals to have eliminated every social-structural basis of dependency. Whatever dependency remains, therefore, can be interpreted as the fault of individuals" (325). With individualization comes the particular blend of emotional constellations associated with neoliberal subjectivity: namely, an enhanced sense of one's own responsibility for oneself, and the forms of self-perfection and self-focus that this requires. Nikolas Rose (1998) expansively analyzes the implications of this form of self-focus for the psy-discourses that dominate contemporary society: the proliferation of self-help manuals and pop psychology that have found a new and lucrative market within neoliberal societies. Of course, responsibility and the efforts of individualized self-actualization come with other forms of emotional baggage: namely, guilt and a sense of failure if one is unable to live up to these neoliberal ideals.

Conclusions

Hannah Arendt (1971) once noted that "absence of thought is not stupidity; it can be found in highly intelligent people, and a wicked heart is not its cause; it is probably the other way around, that wickedness may be caused by absence of thought" (13). Arendt identifies this quality—of thoughtlessness—as lying at the center of any crisis in democracy (see also Young-Bruehl 2006). Arendt was writing long before the ascendancy of neoliberalism, although she was a vocal and concerned critic of some of the qualities of liberal democracy, which she saw as vulnerable to thoughtlessness as an apolitical end (Benhabib 2004). Nonetheless, her call for thoughtfulness as an essential aspect of a functioning public sphere remains cogent and relevant. The possibility for thoughtful, engaged, and ethical political practice remains an issue of enormous concern at the beginning of the twenty-first century, particularly with respect to youth political engagement within the context of neoliberalism, restrictive forms of youth citizenship, and adult-centered social movements.

Were Arendt still alive today, she might well lament the likelihood of the current context for promoting the deeply reflexive thinking, judging, and acting that she saw as central to ethical political conduct. This is not to suggest that youth are not engaged in ethical conduct; rather, it is to highlight how the cultural field within which they must act always already situates them as incapable of such action, making it significantly harder for them to achieve recognition as such. What Arendt (1968/1994) identified as the "right to have rights," whereby the constitution of one's claims to citizenship within the state must first be recognized by that state, is also telling here. Within a cultural and political sphere where young people are discursively, materially, and metaphorically denied access to substantive forms of citizenship, their very possibilities to engage in meaningful political critique whithers, substantially impoverishing the potential for a truly democratic public sphere.

This chapter has traced the essential contradiction contained within the concept of "youth citizenship" in a neoliberal era: if youth are inherently (by definition) dependent, and thus are inherently (by definition) unable to be citizens, and yet dependence has become a term signifying personal failure, what relationship can they then have with the state? In other words, if they are always already mere citizens-in-waiting, structurally positioned as incapable of independence, and yet expected through the governance forces of neoliberalism to become self-regulating, then how can they possibly take up legitimate places as recognizable political actors? The simple response: they can't; or at least, efforts to do so will be met with the ridicule, vapid or hysterical media representations, and overzealous police response that has become the common experience of young people attempting to engage in thoughtful, oppositional activist projects. Such restrictive elements of the cultural sphere within which youth political engagement takes place carries particular implications for the constitution of youth activist subcultures that have sprung up around these oppositional practices. These include historical forms of class and "race" conflict, as well as particular gender dynamics, each in their own way consistent with the long history of "appropriate" citizenship behavior that has been ascribed to youth within liberal and neoliberal democracies. This history is the subject of the next chapter; the subsequent chapters will trace the experiences of young activists themselves, captured through ethnographic methods, as they respond to the particular and peculiar context that this array of influences has created.

2

Constructing the Good Youth Citizen: A History of the Present

> [We must question] customary ways of thinking and acting politically through the radical historicization of everything having to do with democracy: its vocabulary, its official discourse and ordinary representations, its distinctive devices and associations.
> —Wacquant 2005a, 2

The historicized context within which today's youth activists come to their practices consists of almost impossibly complex layers of personal and family histories, regional and national histories, global flows of migration and trade, and multiple other influences and effects. Thus, the task this chapter sets out to achieve is, in many ways, an impossible one: to understand the contemporary construction of Citizen Youth through a history of the present. Nonetheless, this chapter aims to rise to the challenge posed by Wacquant, of historicizing "everything having to do with democracy," including, in this case, the constitution of those individuals who make up a democracy, its citizens. The slice of history the chapter draws on for this task is that of citizenship education as it has evolved within the particular liberal democratic state of Canada. In doing so, I am attempting to answer the question that Hava Gordon (2010) poses within the U.S. context: "[What] role [does] schooling [play] in constructing youth as citizens-in-the-making rather than as actualized political forces in their own right?" (60).

I tackle this question through an interpretive tool adapted from Paul Ricoeur's phenomenological notion of the "detour."

The goal of the Ricoeurian detour (1998) is to provide some reflective space, some objectifying distance (a process he calls "distantiation"), in order to gain insight into the dilemmas and contradictions of the present: "History... explores the field of 'imaginative' variations which surround the present and the real that we take for granted in everyday life" (295). I have added to this a "detour" through a relevant topic from the contemporary moment, that is, the neoliberal elements of recent civics education curricular documents. The purpose of the "detour" is not to suggest some sort of causal relationship between past and present; such an approach would misrepresent the complexity of social realities, and the uneven manner in which history unfolds. Rather, it is to highlight the fact that the "now" does not exist in isolation; it has not sprung from nowhere. If we see that today youth activists are overwhelmingly white and middle class (which will be described in greater detail in the chapters to come), then it is interesting, and relevant, that the "good citizen" of the past has always been valorized as a white and middle-class subject. Likewise, if we see the strains of neoliberal subjectivity within young activists' accounts—through experiences of guilt and particular individualized consumption practices, each described in the chapters to come—it is important to appreciate the wider historical and contemporary context within which such experiences occur. It is not to suggest a predictive capacity of history, but to paint a broader picture, in order to bring a more nuanced appreciation of the multiple influences that shape the present day. As Jocelyn Létourneau (2006) points out, education and its history can become "intellectual crutches" that individuals use to "help them understand the world in its past and present, and to anticipate its future as well" (71). He asks: "How does information of different types mix in a person's mind to produce ways of seeing that, over time, will consolidate in 'mythistories' that may undermine his or her capacity to see the world in another way?" (ibid.). In other words, how have the historical and educational inculcation of values and norms associated with the "good citizen" come to shape the manner in which youth activists are viewed by the world, and view themselves?

The detour that follows is intended to partially reveal the gendered, classed, and racialized aspects of the history of the "good citizen," and link it to the wider cultural pressures to be a particular kind of activist. My task is thus to uncouple the notion of "the activist" from that of an inherently "moral subject," fighting for freedom, democracy, and so on. Instead, I seek within these pages to generate understanding about "the activist" as a deeply gendered, classed and racialized category. This is not to suggest that individual young people engaged in activist practices are not motivated by ideals of freedom, democracy, or morality more generally; however, my argument is that those who are able to *take up* this identity are located as such within a specific class, gender and "race" imaginary (as well as, in different although connected ways, an imaginary influenced by assumptions about ability and sexuality). What I hope to reveal through this section of the book is the long history of morality claims by the state about the "good citizen" that have always been inextricably linked to dominant concepts of "normalcy" and all of its classed, raced, and gendered baggage.

Detour: The Cultural Space of the Canadian "Good Citizen"

This historical detour begins with the inception of Canadian public schooling in 1847, which spread rapidly across the disparate colonies that would soon become Canada. Its primary goal: to instill patriotism within young people, where schools were intended to be a homogenizing force that would create "good Canadian citizens" in the image of British loyalists (Joshee 2004).[1] Arising on the heels of the political uprisings within Lower and Upper Canada of 1837 and 1838, schooling was seen by those in power to be one way to ensure the maintenance of civil order through cultivating students' "sense of citizenship, loyalty, respect for property, and deference to authority" (Axelrod 1997, 25). Even prior to this period, civic education appeared as a central component of educational endeavors in Upper Canada (which roughly mapped onto the future province of Ontario; DiMascio 2010). Those advocating for compulsory school attendance in the mid-nineteenth century—which would be implemented in almost all of the provinces by 1871—based their argument on the belief that there was a fundamental lack among young people of the time of "public spirit, of collective energy, and enterprise" (Prentice 1999, 47). This early period of broad-based education within Canada took place at a time when the pressures of nation-building were at a particular high. In 1867, Confederation brought together the four original colonies—Nova Scotia, New Brunswick, Quebec, and Ontario—under one national state. Not long after, in 1871, British Columbia also entered Confederation, the same year that it implemented a free-school system (Axelrod 1997).[2] Schooling was understood as one way to build and perfect a Canadian nation that would be second to none on the world stage of nations (Prentice 1999). Such efforts were perhaps nowhere more fraught than in attempts to align the French-speaking population of Quebec (formerly Lower Canada) with the British values of the English-speaking majority in the rest of Canada (Curtis 2003).

It was also a time during which the colonial power of Britain continued to hold substantial sway, both ideologically and through the choice of textbooks and schooling systems. Patrick Walsh (2008) documents the development and dispersal of textbooks used in two British colonies between the 1850s and 1870s: Ireland and Upper Canada. As Walsh notes, "the 'universalist' discourse of the administrative arm of the British Empire was what made these books so peculiarly suitable for use in Ireland and Ontario" (649). The textbooks reified, and conveyed to a mass audience of children and parents alike, "the 'ideal' of the nation within the imperial disposition as it was conceived by the colonial elites which administered its political and social instruments" (645). This imperial disposition took the shape of relentless promotion of the values of the British (read: Anglo-Saxon protestant) middle classes, and an equally relentless disdain for any who had not been fortunate enough to be exposed to the benefits of their colonial reach. Walsh illustrates this point through the following excerpts from the texts that were jointly used in Ireland and Ontario:

> ["New Holland," now Australia] is inhabited by a race of savages who are among the lowest and most degraded that are to be found in the world. One of the things that formerly prevented the settlers from going into the interior, was the violent opposition met from the savages, who came in great numbers, armed with their long spears, against those who were so courageous as to attempt to penetrate into unknown parts of the country; but they are now more amicably disposed towards newcomers...
>
> South of the great desert [i.e., the Sahara], the nations are all black, and though differing from each other, all belong to the negro race. Some negroes have black skins, short, black, curly and woolly hair, with black eyes, flat noses, and thick lips. They are certainly an ugly race, but when educated and well-treated, they are found to be kind and good-natured, faithful to their protectors, and as well skilled in whatever art or trade they have learnt, as Europeans are. All the negro nations of Africa are idolaters and in a state of great ignorance and barbarism...

Such horrifyingly racist depictions were mirrored by educational policies that resulted in significant and largely successful attempts to suppress, segregate, and assimilate Aboriginal peoples and various ethnic minorities. For example, Canadian Blacks, themselves either the descendents of slaves brought to Nova Scotia and Upper Canada in the 1750s, or escaped slaves from the United States, were normally educated in segregated Black-only schools, supported by legislation that was officially on the books until 1964 (Axelrod 1997). Chinese students in British Columbia were forced into segregated schools, because they were thought to represent a moral, intellectual, social, and health threat to the other (white) students (Stanley 2002).

For Aboriginal peoples, the concept of citizenship was an explicitly exclusionary one, and mainstream schooling historically misrepresented and maligned the realities of their culture and identity (as it largely continues to do today; Battiste & Semaganis 2002; Persson 1986). The education of Aboriginal peoples throughout Canada's history has been marked by an emphasis on either "civilizing" or assimilating them to meet the moral imperatives of the European settlers' norms (Frideres 1978). Such aims were carried out, in part, through the establishment of Residential Schools, which were used to separate Aboriginal children from their families and extinguish all traces of their Aboriginal culture, including their language. The perception of Aboriginal peoples that shaped these schools are reflected in this statement made by an inspector of schools in the mid-1800s:

> Little can be done with (the Indian child). He can be taught to do a little at farming, and at stock raising, and to dress in a more civilized manner, but that is all. The child who goes to a day school learns little and what he learns is soon forgotten, while his tastes are fashioned at home, and his inherited aversion to toil is in no way combatted. (As cited in Kirkness & Bowman 1992, 10)

Aboriginal peoples were thus seen as outside of the redemptive status of citizenship, capable only of menial labor, and in dire need of "civilizing." Indeed, the government made it legally impossible for an "Indian" to become a citizen of Canada; if an Aboriginal person did manage to conform to mainstream notions of success within Canadian schooling, and proceeded to university or attained a profession, the Canadian government would remove the government-inscribed category of "Indian" from that person, and allow him (rarely, if ever, her) the right of enfranchisement (Coates 1999).

Timothy Stanley (2006) provides an eloquent example of the multifaceted exclusions incorporated into the "public memory" of the Canadian nation-state—a memory constituted by mass media, museums, and public school curricula, among other relevant sites (37). He describes a survey distributed by the Dominion Institute that "shows how easy it is for taken-for-granted categories to create exclusions." One question asks "in what decade in the twentieth century were Canadian women given the right to vote in elections?":

> Here the answer being looked for is the 1910's. [T]his answer appears to make complete sense as it is indeed in this decade

that the federal government and most provinces extended voting rights at general elections to women for the first time since 1867. However, in fact, this answer reduces "Canadians" to English speaking people of European origins. Women in Quebec got the right to vote in 1940, but in the logic of this question and answer they apparently are not "Canadian." Nor are the Chinese, Japanese, and South Asian women "Canadian" who (along with their menfolk) got the right to vote federally and in certain provinces only in 1947–9. Nor, presumably, are the women "Canadian" who were so-called Status Indians and who did not get the right to vote federally until 1960, when all "status Indians" did. Similarly, the category "Canadian women" apparently does not include the women of the Iroquois Confederacy, who had been voting since at least the thirteenth century, only to have this right taken away by the Canadian government in the twentieth. (37)

This eloquent example, excerpted at length here, illustrates the manner in which "common sense" notions of citizenship, belonging, and inclusion are reproduced, not only through schooling but also through other institutions of public memory that draw upon and corroborate the evidence provided within the public school system. These "common sense" understandings become the cultural backdrop against which young people must compare themselves as they work out their own relationship to the state, often as dissident citizens (Sparks 1997).

Another issue of deep concern to Canadian elites who developed the public school system was the impact of class differences in society. As Alison Prentice (1999) notes, education was seen as one way to "prevent the poor from robbing or murdering the rich" (67). Schooling was perceived as a means through which to ensure the "respectability" of the poor and working classes, where respectability meant mimicking the affects of the middle classes: "refined manners and taste, respectable religion, proper speech and, finally, [in English Canada] the ability to read and write proper English" (68). It was understood as a peacemaking institution, whereby the implementation of free education would bring the classes together to be bound by the experience of being schooled side-by-side (Prentice 1999). To this end, although schooling was explicitly concerned with the development of good Canadian citizens who were loyal to the state, such democratic practices as public debate and disagreement were discouraged, and in their place Christian love, order, and correct social behavior were thought to ensure social cohesion (ibid.). As noted by Alison Prentice, "[Schools and] approved textbooks were designed to spread the doctrine of social harmony and progress, and to ignore or suppress the facts of social and political conflict" (128). Thus the good citizen of this period was the obedient, loyal, respectable individual of middle-class comportment, if not middle-class social position.

By the middle of the twentieth century, discourses of citizenship had not substantially shifted, continuing to rely on classed and raced indicators of "normalcy" and Christian morality. Working-class people in the decades between 1920 and 1965 were expected to demonstrate their "good citizenship" through "their own moral propriety and dedications to the work ethic, or...their churchgoing and wholesome leisure activities" (Sangster 2002, 350). Within Canadian schooling, discourses of normalcy—constructed along lines of gender, class, "race," and sexual conformity—penetrated every aspect of young people's education. Mary Louise Adams (1997) points to an educational film—*Are You Popular?*—first produced in 1947 and updated in 1958. She describes it as follows:

> To make its point the film contrasts Ginny and Caroline. Ginny is the unpopular girl, packaged in multiple working-class signifiers. Her jewellery is big and gaudy, her clothes are fussy, her hair is too old for her age, she "yoo-hoos" the other kids in the cafeteria. And, we find out from the solemn-toned male narrator, she goes parking with boys at night. Caroline, on the other hand, is very popular, in an easy kind of way (which is, of course, the right way). She is dressed simply. She greets her friends calmly and pleasantly. She is "interested in girls rather than boys." She offers to help with the school play. She does not "park" with boys in their cars. She will, however, go on a date with a boy if it is okay with her mother. She will be home before an agreed-upon curfew. And, when she and her date arrive home, mother will greet them with a tray of fresh brownies. For both Caroline and Ginny, class, moral character, and popularity are indivisible. (90)

Such educational endeavors reinscribed gendered and sexualized norms upon young people in Canadian schools. They carried within them the gendered and moral subtexts of "citizenship," providing a range of examples of how one must shape oneself within the bounds of "normal." Such expressions of normalcy were, of course, also profoundly heterosexual. Queer bodies had no place in a mainstream classroom, much as they do not today. As Becki Ross (1998) notes, those who professed or acted upon same-sex desire could never be included as "fully fledged members or citizens of the Canadian nation. Rather, they were perceived as dangerous, sick, potential criminals and improperly socialized deviants" (193).

The postwar era also saw the emergence of a new impulse toward "progressive" education, inspired by the work of American philosopher John Dewey. Brian Low (2003) documents how progressive education and the mental hygiene movement were captured within films produced by the National Film Board of Canada during this period. Low notes that the main goal of the mental hygiene movement was "to forge a "new generation" of young people whose childhood development would be guided by scientific research and whose adulthood, therefore, would be happier, more productive, and more self-reliant than any generation before them" (541). This might be seen as the early progenitor of the contemporary neoliberal citizen (described in greater detail later), the self-regulating subject whose ultimate citizenship project is to make oneself "happy" rather than to participate in a democratic public sphere (see also Rose 1999).

The 1960s marked the apex of the social citizen (Marshall 1992/1950), when the government promised to support and provide for *all* Canadians through the provisions of the social welfare state (Brodie 2002).[3] It was a period of intensive reflection on core Canadian values, identity, and national unity, in an effort to describe "who we are." This coincided with the rise of Quebec nationalism and separatism, rapid immigration that was beginning to noticeably shift the population from a white settler society to a multiracial and multiethnic society, and the intensification of globalization (ibid.). Immigration policy became less explicitly racist after 1967; however, the implementation of a point system that rated immigrants on the basis of their "skills" served to reinforce disadvantages faced by potential immigrants on the basis of class, gender, and geographic location (which is often connected to "race"/ethnicity) (Abu-Laban 1998). Although immigrants were granted admission on the basis of skills, citizenship in Canada still did not offer equal access to social, political, and economic parity (DePass & Qureshi 2002; Mata 2002). To this day, visible minority groups in Canada, and immigrants in particular, continue to be subject to higher rates of unemployment, lower incomes even if they are employed, and greater likelihood of working at manual labor jobs than the rest of the population (Mata 2002).

The recessions and oil shocks of the 1970s witnessed a shift from a commitment to social welfare for *all* Canadians to become a focus only on those *in need*, whereby the rest of the country's citizens were expected to "sacrifice when times were tough" (Brodie 2002, 61). The 1980 Speech from the Throne declared that "Canadians will accept sacrifice" and they understand that "the state cannot meet every demand or satisfy every group" (as cited in ibid.). This marked the beginning of an ever-growing emphasis on individual over state responsibility for citizen well-being, one of the hallmarks of neoliberalism. Although little has been written on Canadian education from this period, with even less on citizenship education, the available research suggests that this was a period of contestation between the emerging "progressivism" within education (with its own roots within the social gospel movement and Deweyan democratic educational philosophy; Titley 1990) and the "back-to-basics" call of those hoping to return to a more standardized, traditional manner of schooling (Titley and Mazurek 1990). Education at this time also came to be seen more explicitly as a form of investment, developing "human capital" in order to compete in the expanding technological markets. Federal government spending on higher education increased dramatically, reflecting this shifting state priority (Titley and Mazurek 1990). As Titley and Mazurek note, "The result of all this was a veritable mania for education throughout the 1960s and into the first half of the 1970s. Between 1960 and 1975 national expenditure on education at all levels rose from $1,706,000,000 to $12,228,000,000—a seven-fold increase" (115).

The result, not surprisingly, was higher retention rates; whereas only 35 percent of students had completed high school in 1961, that number rose to 75 percent in 1976 (ibid.). However, this increase did not necessarily translate into an increase in equality of opportunity. As J. R. Young (1990) notes, "What we may be doing is simply spending an increasingly larger portion of the gross national product to increase the disparity between those who receive the greatest rewards, both financial and social, and those who receive the least" (166).

The focus on progressivism within education, though short-lived, reached its zenith during this period. This shift was heralded by the emergence of a plethora of reports on education in the late 1960s and early 1970s. These reports were "inspired by the ideas of every progressive writer from Rousseau to Dewey, [and] exuded unbounded optimism regarding the potential benefits of its pedagogical prognosis. The approach [they] advocated would benefit all children and foster equal opportunity while combating ignorance, poverty, and prejudice" (Titley and Mazurek 1990, 116). It was during this period that standardized exams began to be phased out, and alternative schools began to appear. Multiculturalism as an official government policy also appeared during this period, and was promptly incorporated into schooling (Mazurek and Kach 1990). This period was experienced as an opportunity for greater flexibility and autonomy for teachers, and the incorporation of more nontraditional subjects into education (Titley and Mazurek 1990); this presumably included opportunities for incorporating alternative, non-normative conceptions of citizenship into everyday practices of schooling and curriculum.

The expansive optimism and experimentation of the period soon came to an end, however. By the 1970s, most of the alternative schools were either abandoned or absorbed into the public school system (ibid.). New reports were being issued that suggested the schools needed to return to the traditional curriculum emphases that had been briefly dislocated in the 1960s. Much of the perceived educational malaise was blamed on teachers, and standardized exams began to be reinstituted.

As Titley and Mazurek suggest, "economic recession was the principal culprit for the descent from the clouds" (119).

By the late 1990s and early millennium, an increasing anxiety about the capacity and willingness of young people to participate in the nation-state emerged, both in Canada and across other Western liberal democratic states. Thought to be captured by statistics documenting dropping voter turnout among those under the age of thirty-five (Institute for Public Policy Research 2006; Pammett & LeDuc 2003), the response to this perceived inadequacy among young people has been a recent surge in citizenship education (Best 2003; Ichilov 2005; Levinson 2003). Such initiatives have taken a wide-ranging array of approaches, including global education, civics education, and character education. In the Canadian context, almost every province and territory has introduced a new citizenship education course in the last decade, including the three provinces that are home to my research participants. British Columbia introduced a new Civics 11 curriculum in 2005, one of three optional credits that students can take to complete their social science requirement; in Ontario, the new Civics 10 came into effect in 2002, and is a required course for all grade 10 students; in Quebec, the new History and Citizenship education module was introduced as part of the social sciences curriculum in 2004.

In order to assess contemporary claims being made about the "good citizen," I conducted a discourse analysis of these three civics curriculum documents. My analysis revealed an emphasis on citizenship responsibility over rights, and the requirement of individuals to become self-regulating by becoming "informed" and being "ethical."[4] While such an emphasis may seem harmless at first glance, and is certainly congruent with Canada's image of itself as a humanitarian liberal democracy, an issue of concern emerges when it is noted how quickly the concept of "citizenship" is coupled with the cautionary words "responsible," "ethical," and "informed." These couplets suggest that citizenship might only be taken up by those reasonable and responsible individuals who take the time to deliberate on all aspects of a social issue before taking action. It certainly does little to inform individuals about their rights and entitlements as citizens within the state (i.e., to education, health care, welfare). Instead, the form of subjectivity implied by civics curricula is the model of the desirable citizen within the context of neoliberal states, whose qualities include endless self-scrutiny, an individualized focus on one's personal development over and above the well-being of the collective, and the capacity to continually renegotiate one's skills and identity in light of the demands of global capitalism (Mitchell 2003; Raco 2003; Rose 1999). I would suggest that the repeated emphasis throughout all three curricular documents on both "responsibility" and "informed citizenship" represents the continuation of a discursive shift of the burdens of citizenship onto the individual, through the constant reiteration of the requirement to be self-regulating and self-scrutinizing. The repeated return to the notion of "responsibility" becomes the ultimate individual, self-reflexive burden of the citizen in neoliberal times.

Detour Completed: Back to the Present

The intent of this "detour" has been to illuminate the ways in which elite priorities, state ordering of identity categories, and social exclusion are implicated in the story of the Canadian nation, the result being that profoundly moral claims have always shaped the idea of the "citizen." Through this process, I have tried to provoke questions about how we can begin to uncover and think through the morality claims made by the state, and understand the links these carry to young people's classification struggles (Bourdieu 1984; see also Kennelly & Dillabough 2008)—in other words, to understand how the notion of the "good citizen" is deeply classed, raced, and gendered, and how these aspects are mobilized by young people attempting to work out their relationship to each other and to the nation-state itself. The participants who will be represented in subsequent chapters are both products of this state, and are also attempting to resist its impacts. The history of the "good citizen" and its link to action within the public sphere nonetheless make their appearance within the stories that the activists tell—their *moral claims* about themselves and those around them can never be entirely separated from this context. This is not to suggest that the young people of this study are *created* by this history in any straightforward causal relationship—rather, it is to acknowledge and assess the historical and cultural spaces through which individuals must pass before coming to their own sense of the world, and to recognize the inextricable nature of state claims about "the good" as a cultural manifestation with material impacts. This is the detour's intended use: to shed light on aspects of the present in a manner that reveals hitherto unconsidered linkages and possibilities.

The rest of the book shall be devoted to recounting and analyzing some of the complex interactions that make up young people's experiences of, and within, the nation-state. While such experiences are neither straightforward nor predictable, they *do* follow particular patterns—always with exceptions, never immutable, but with patterns nonetheless. It is my concern here to trace these patterns, drawing links between what I have witnessed and been told by participants with a larger theoretical conception of the role of the state and culture in relation to the everyday. My ultimate aim is *not* to indict the young people with whom I carried out this research, somehow laying the blame on their shoulders for "capitulating" to state and cultural stories about the raced, classed, gendered, and liberal/neoliberal self, but rather to demonstrate the ways in which we are all susceptible to, and regulated by, the powerful claims about belonging and citizenship to which we are subjected through a wide array of cultural formations. I trace these connections between culture, history, citizenship, "race," class, gender, and activism as one way of providing some critical space between the fraught and necessary practices of activism and the lived experiences of young people who become so engaged with the concept of political action.[5]

3

Good Citizen/Bad Activist: The Cultural Role of the State in Youth Political Participation

The previous chapters have traced the particular relationships among youth, citizenship, neoliberalism, and state claims about the "good citizen" as revealed through the lens of citizenship education. This chapter now begins the process of drawing these disparate theoretical and historical pieces together, through a detailed exploration of what I am calling the "cultural role of the state" on youth activists, as captured through ethnographic methods. Stuart Hall (1985) suggests that the state, as a concept, cannot be understood as a monolithic entity with straightforward intentions that can be read off without contradiction. Nonetheless, he argues, "the State remains one of the crucial sites in a modern capitalist social formation where political practices of different kinds are condensed" (93). Understood through the language of governance, and highly consistent with Foucault's governmentality approach outlined in chapter one, Hall's formulation suggests that there are a range of cultural mediators that function together in order to generate a consistent set of ideas that people take up as the "common sense" or "right way to be." That such "common sense" then tends to coincide with state ideals is the core enigma of state-and-culture interactions, largely because these cultural influences are pervasive and often difficult to discern. According to Raymond Williams (1989), culture is like the air we breathe—its presence is taken for granted and thus is generally not noticed, something we simply live with and through, usually without thinking about it. The ways in which culture shapes our experience of the world is thus difficult to explain; the ways in which culture shapes our experience of the *nation-state* is particularly elusive.

One of the central dilemmas that this book is attempting to address is the contradictory and yet complementary relationship that appears to currently exist between the "young activist" and the "young citizen." Given the elusive nature of culture—as the air we breathe—it is sometimes only possible to catch glimpses of the underlying tensions and misrepresentations through sideways glances. For example, take the image with which this book opened, of a young bloody-faced activist being dragged away by riot police. What impact does such an image have on young people? What spaces of interpretation does it open up and foreclose through its presence on the front page of one of Canada's two national daily newspapers? Jonathon[1] (age twenty-five) suggests that images such as this one contribute to what he called "the stigma of activism":

> *Jonathon*: Like I'm totally reacting to a stereotype, right? So I'm totally an example of how the system is working. Right? It's really interesting. But if I were to create a stereotype [of an activist], it would be someone at a protest, wearing a bandana or some you know, political propaganda, whether it be a Mao t-shirt or Che Guevara t-shirt. A lot of the color red... The media loves that image.

Such images become part of a larger cultural conversation, one that takes place on many fronts and coheres into a sedimented set of social perceptions about specific actors, not necessarily based in the realities of social experiences. In other words, they become part of the "common sense" that constitutes the cultural space within which contemporary activism takes place. From my field notes, documenting a conversation I had with one of my own family members:

> [I had a] brief conversation with Simon on Sunday, during which he asked me about my research. As I began to describe it, struggling to find the words that would make sense to this middle-aged doctor who once proclaimed to me that his

affluent American lifestyle was just the way life was supposed to be, I found myself saying that I was studying youth activists, then, somewhat wryly, adding, "you know, rabble rousers." His 11-year-old daughter walked in at this point and asked what a youth activist was, and Simon said, laughing somewhat but I think being serious, "trouble makers."

I was, of course, participating in wider cultural scripts about activism by using "rabble-rousers" in order to breach the "common sense barrier" that lay between me and this relative of mine, who lives in a very different world from the one with which I am familiar. These examples are meant to illustrate the depth of reach that these cultural codes have, and how they can serve to uphold and reinforce particular ideas. Understanding young activists as "rabble-rousers," "trouble-makers," or out-of-control maniacs constantly on the verge of arrest is one very powerful way in which the cultural sphere can reinforce for young people their own compliance with the conventional liberal democratic ideals offered as the only reasonable way to participate in democracy in Canada.

One of the key concepts through which I understand young people's experiences of the broader cultural sphere is that of Raymond Williams' (1977) *structures of feeling*. This concept attests to the manner in which young activists encounter the state and related cultural influences through emotional experiences and anxieties—things that appear as personal dramas but which are not that (Bourdieu 1999). Such emotional responses, in turn, play a role in shaping their capacity to participate within the public realm. That is, they experience the norms reinforced by the state and the cultural sphere bodily and emotionally, and must continually navigate this cultural realm in order to maintain the identity of "activist." Williams' concept provides one way to situate the expressed emotions of young activists as emerging not from within the bodies of individualized subjects separated from their social context (e.g. as psychological), but as a window into the larger structures that they encounter and navigate on a daily basis (see also Dillabough et al. 2008). The compromises and negotiations that young activists must engage in can be accompanied by a "psychic cost" (Lucey & Reay 2002) that takes its toll in the form of self-doubt and anxiety. These emotional responses, taken together, form part of the analysis in this chapter, of how young people encounter and navigate the claims made within both the state and the broader cultural sphere about activism and the requirements of the contemporary "good citizen."

Performing Activism, Becoming Citizens

The manner in which state histories, morality claims, and neoliberal cultural norms intersect to create specific opportunities and limits for young activists became strongly apparent to me during one particular day of my Toronto fieldwork. I had attended two events as part of my ethnographic research, the first a speech by Craig Kielburger, the second a memorial organized by the Ontario Coalition Against Poverty (OCAP). While each position themselves as "anti-poverty activists," their approaches to activism, and the responses they received from police and the general public, mark the tensions that exist between the idea of the "good citizen" and the "bad activist." Kielburger, well known for starting the organization "Free the Children" at the age of twelve, was speaking at the University of Toronto about how young people might engage in community projects to help combat poverty in the Global South. Remarkable within his lecture was his repeated emphasis on the benefits of such activism for the people so engaged. For example, he noted that activism would make an individual feel good about himself or herself, generating an endorphin rush similar to a "runner's high." He also reiterated the difference one could make through shifting consumption patterns; for example, he suggested that poverty could be eradicated if everyone were to donate money to charitable causes rather than purchase perfume. Finally, he suggested that audience members could make a difference by purchasing his t-shirt and book, with his logo "Me to We." The form of citizenship Kielburger offers has been eagerly lauded within citizenship education curricula—for instance, he is given as one example of a "model citizen" within the BC curricula (British Columbia Ministry of Education 2005, 55). He has also been highly visible in his support for a new "character education" curricula (often seen as interchangeable with civics education) in Ontario (Media release 2006).

The OCAP memorial service, on the other hand, consisted of direct criticism of municipal, provincial, and federal levels of government, and their failure to act to protect individuals against the ravages of poverty within Canada. Rather than being in a warm and well-lit university auditorium, this event took place on a street corner outside the site of a former squat,[2] and was heavily surveilled by police in cars, on horseback, and on foot. The memorial was for Vasyl, a man who had committed suicide after being denied immigrant status, being injured in an unregulated work site, and being forcibly evicted from the squat by police. The OCAP event stands in sharp contrast to Kielburger's depiction of activism as built on consumer choices and self-development. Rather, OCAP's memorial for Vasyl challenged processes of social erasure increasingly created by a neoliberal and economically stratified state. They did this by memorializing a man who had been marginalized (literally to death) within its structures. For their efforts, they received heavy surveillance by the state through its police presence.

Both events were attended by young people concerned about injustices in the world, but each had very different messages about what it means to take action to create positive social change, and what this means for one's relation to the Canadian state. Whereas Kielburger's version of activist-citizenship relies on the consuming citizen engaging in community voluntarism that will allow him or her to feel better about himself or herself, OCAP's version directly challenges state policies that originally created the injustices. The former is applauded as the actions of a "good citizen" (who engages in worthwhile community projects that can resemble activism) whereas the latter precipitates forms of surveillance that suggest it has been carried out by the "bad activist" (who steps beyond the bounds of good citizenship to challenge state claims to legitimacy). It is no coincidence that the former is also highly reconcilable with the neoliberal model of the self-perfecting citizen, through its relentless focus on the individual benefits that accrue to someone performing these versions of activism (e.g., an endorphin rush) and its focus on individualized consumption as the path to social change (e.g., not purchasing perfume).

Each of these strands can be found in other contemporary influences on young people in Canada, including schooling but also extending to other sites. Participants remarked upon the manner in which schools encouraged community engagement, largely consistent with Kielburger's message. They understood that such community involvement had come to be conflated with the idea of good (and successful) citizenship. Nancy (age twenty) made the following remark:

> *Nancy*: The school did encourage participation in extracurricular activities, universities required it, or highly recommended a portfolio that included community participation and a lot of non-academic criteria like that. So those were definitely incentives. To get involved and stuff like that. And it was just part of the portfolio of a good student, that even though [one] succeeds academically but [one also succeeds] otherwise.

Nancy noted that her community involvement was recognized and encouraged by the school as one manner in which to enhance her chances of getting a good position at a university, and that this, unsurprisingly, acted as an incentive to her own participation. To be a "good student" was to be not only academically successful, but also successfully engaged in projects of "good citizenship" such as benevolent community work. Official school documents reinforce this perception; for example, Ontario and BC graduation requirements currently include "community work," which are often explicitly linked to the development of citizenship attributes (British Columbia Ministry of Education 2007; Ontario Ministry of Training, Colleges and Universities 2006).

Recall from the "detour" in the previous chapter that schooling originated as a means to ensure the productive coexistence of conflicting classes and that public dissent and debate were discouraged. Consider then what happens to activism when community involvement is encouraged as a means to enhance one's status as a "good citizen," and when such community involvement is encouraged as forms of "activism." Rajinder (age thirteen) describes one relevant consequence:

> *Rajinder*: So but then, and kind of coming back to that whole problematic term [of activist], because it's a term that's so kind of friendly now, that oh you know, that it's a good thing rather than something that would be threatening or dangerous to the state. Like that's why I know a lot of terms like insurgent or radical have been used by people because those are terms that they don't like to hear, that have been demonized. And, so yeah. So there's this whole friendliness of the term [activism].

The "activism" promoted by Craig Kielburger and the related community work encouraged by schools are examples of how "good citizenship" has come to incorporate certain, although by no means all, aspects of activist practice. While on the one hand appearing to legitimate certain forms of activist practice, and thus perhaps even widening their scope and reach, the gradual conflation of "good citizenship" with certain kinds of activism also functions to undermine the very role of activism, particularly if it involves challenges to the state. Not surprisingly, state interests are generally not aligned with supporting and maintaining practices that challenge them. Arguably, then, the gradual conflation of activism with good citizenship may be one means by which activism is regulated, becoming fundamentally less dangerous in its capacity to intervene into state practices (see also Brown 2005).

It is important not to overstate the degree to which contemporary schooling encourages young people to engage in activist-like practices. Indeed, the vast majority of participants experienced schooling for citizenship as highly irrelevant to their own activism, in part because formal citizenship education retains a strong focus on traditional forms of state engagement from within liberal democracy, such as voting and participation in political parties. The assessment offered by Caleb (age twenty), reflecting on the Ontario curriculum, is typical of many respondents:

> *Caleb*: We have a civics class, it's half a year in grade 10 and it's totally useless...It goes over Canadian government and citizenship and things like that...I think the idea was the

government wanted [the students] to be educated before they could vote. It was also really boring. It was a boring class. So I mean, there was that. It wasn't very inspirational. And it wasn't about being part of something or you know working—it didn't have any sort of focus on you know, so you've now learned about the Canadian government. You can get out there and do your thing. It was more about this is the Canadian government, this is the, you know, powerful people. These are our prime ministers.

From British Columbia, Andrew (age twenty-eight) similarly noted the irrelevance of citizenship education to his development as a politically engaged individual:

> *Andrew*: You have the vague memories of the boring social studies class. You learn you have this political system. There might have been like a mock election in there, which is mildly interesting. But not really because I remember, this is grade eleven or something. They didn't let you, you were given a party and then you had to say why this party was the best. But I was pretty sure that, you know, my family was NDP [National Democratic Party, the left-leaning political party in Canada] and they made the most sense to me. That's who I cheered for in the elections, so. That's who I wanted to be. Or even Green Party. I think I was already thinking Green Party would be a good, but that wasn't allowed, so I remember being irritated by that. No, they never, I don't remember anything in terms of citizenship as I think of it now. It's just sort of citizens are people who live in Canada for long enough and you get a thing and yeah. Nothing memorable anyway.

Participants' general disdain for citizenship education was one of the most consistent results of my interviews, so much so that I began to feel embarrassed when I asked them about their experiences of citizenship education. Their experiences consistently illustrated the ideological undercurrents of civics curricula, highly influenced by histories of liberalism and associated ideas about appropriate limits to citizen participation within the state. As Westheimer and Kahne (2003) note, "the narrow and often ideologically conservative conception of citizenship embedded in many current efforts at teaching for democracy reflects neither arbitrary choices nor pedagogical limitations but rather political choices with political consequences" (1). One political consequence of liberalism's influence is that it can foreclose discussion about other possible visions for democracy. Farah (age twenty-seven) notes:

> *Farah*: More and more so lately I think democracy is a really stupid thing. I think it's mythical. It's like as a political objective—like the fact that we're selling democracy [to] the rest of the world—not like when we're shoving it down people's throats but when people are seriously dying for the right to vote and stuff, I just can't believe the way we've sold our model of democracy as being something really engaged and progressive because it pretty much ends debate—our model of it, at least you know? The idea [that] a system of people voting could make anything like—I don't know, again it's arrogant to tell people living under a serious, brutal military style dictatorship that the right to vote is over-rated, but—I mean what's worse? Living with the option between two or three CEOs you know? And really not having a say. Like that very option or structure making people so apathetic that—yeah.

Farah's analysis of Canadian democracy provides a different genesis for the youth "apathy" and lack of involvement that has served as the rationale for developing new civics curricula in the twenty-first century. Rather than seeing the problem as lying primarily within the citizens themselves, she sees the very structure of democracy within Canada to be limited such that people ultimately find participation within it to be meaningless. She further identifies the problem as lying within ever-increasing degrees of class stratification and inequality:

> *Farah*: I don't know what the statistics are right now about the poor underclass in Canada but I think somehow we think everyone has an iPod or something and I don't really think everyone does—I think most people don't. And I think there's a giant poor population that thinks that there's not as many of them as they think. Because...images of [former Prime Minister] Paul Martin and stuff make you think that there's a general middle class vibe in the country or something...I just think it's paralyzing and it makes people not do anything.

Neoliberal Subjects

Farah's analysis is echoed by contemporary scholars who have critiqued liberal democracy, and the rights it is supposed to protect, as less a development of freedom "than of an increasingly administered society—a civil society of bureaucratic agencies and a civic currency of proceduralism and litigiousness" (Brown 2001, 12; see also Foucault 1994a; Marcuse 1991/1964). Within liberal (and neoliberal) democratic states, the individual is only able to interact with the state through his or her individual acts, most primarily voting. Bourdieu (2005) notes that the act of voting strips the decision-making process from any intimation of social interaction or mutual accountability:

> The liberal vision identifies the elementary act of democracy as it is ordinarily conceived with the solitary, nay silent and secret, action of individuals... [B]y bringing into existence, on a specific day, the succession of individuals who "pass one after another before the ballot box" and by suspending "for a moment," just long enough to make a choice, all social bonds, between husband and wife, father and son, employer and employee, priest and parishioner, teacher and pupil... it reduces groups to a detotalized series of individuals whose "opinion" will never be more than a statistical aggregation of individual opinions individually expressed. (57)

In other words, voting has come to represent a kind of economic rationality that sees democracy as the aggregate result of individual choices (or purchases) within the political marketplace. One consequence of such an individualized vision of democracy, and of one's relation to the state, is a particular structure of feeling that manifests within youth activist subcultures as an overwhelming burden of individualized responsibility and its powerful psychic associate, guilt. This is further complicated by the forces of governmentality that have emerged around neoliberal ideals, specifically an inexorable focus on the individual and the individual's capacity (and requirement) to make the best of his or her own life. This "self-perfecting" subject is bombarded with messages about how to live well and be happy, with the suggestion that achieving such self-actualization is equivalent to fulfilling any political or ethical obligations that he or she might have (Rose 1999, cf. 166). In other words, activism, as it is expressed and experienced within twenty-first century Canada, has largely become a form of self-realization, just as has voting.

The larger pressures for such self-actualization are manifested within the cultural realm through, to name a few examples, the proliferation of self-help marketing techniques and the vast expansion of psycho-therapeutic regimes (Rose 1999). It is experienced by young people as a requirement for reflexivity that can be overwhelming:

> *Vincent* (age twenty-six): But, yeah. In terms of that responsibility? I don't know. I mean, I guess there needs to be some kind of a sense of empathy, like a greater empathy to at least be able to track, you know, a crying Palestinian kid on TV back to yourself sitting in your living room, being able to kind of have an awareness of how that kid is sort of related to what you do when you go out on the street and do your work everyday, live your life and you know?...So in that sense maybe it's like an extreme or even pathological self-awareness. Like a constant self-awareness.

As Vincent notes, among the many relevant messages directed toward Canadian young people is that their individual development depends to a certain degree on their capacity to understand and help others, particularly those located elsewhere in the world. This is imagined within the wider cultural realm to result in both feeling better about oneself while simultaneously strengthening one's CV (and thus making oneself more marketable in the competitive global economy). Such an individualized focus on one's possible "contribution" to the world (as opposed to *participation* within a community) has problematic ramifications. For example, it can act to convert the human capacity for solidarity and compassion to an essentializing reflex that does little to rectify the very complex social, economic, and political problems that trouble the vast majority of the world's population. It thus can act to distance, rather than build, genuine human connections, particularly in how it plays out within our contemporary liberal and neoliberal milieu, with its specific messages about what it means to be a "good citizen." In essence, such an individualized approach to social justice and democracy serves to erode the "web of relations" that Hannah Arendt (1998) cites as central to a functioning public sphere.

That powerful cultural messages about their responsibility to the "world," writ large, were deeply felt and honored by young activists was evident from participants' reflections on their early sense of wanting to work toward social change:

> *Minna* (age twenty-three): And I remember, uh, there was this environmental club that was somehow connected to Safeway?—I don't really remember, but, these stickers were pivotal for me! It was a picture of the globe, and kids can save the world, it was this mini-campaign that they had started, I'm not sure where it came from. But it was, to me it's a real marker of where it started.
>
> *Andrew*: And so in a way it'd be like well we're not going to be like that. We're going to do something different and have an impact on the world.
>
> *Daniel* (age twenty-one): I always wanted to change the world, you know?
>
> *Carolyn* (age twenty): It made me realize that I can change the world.

Such sentiments, highly consistent with the wider cultural pressures to be a particular kind of "good citizen," need to be understood as a specific cultural phenomenon happening within high modern, individualizing times, within a country that holds a dominant position in global power relations. Thus the professed desire to "change the world," generally expressed as a childhood aspiration, partially reveals the specific parameters of youth activism within Canada—as an individualized phenomenon that obliterates the interconnections between Canada and the "world" of which it is a part. It also becomes part of a structure of feeling such that the prevalent cultural claims about what it is to be a "good person" (or citizen) becomes associated with grandiose impossibilities (set up to fail): to "save the world."

What are the implications and consequences of such a widespread articulation of the possibilities for social change? By individualizing social change struggles, it is easy to slip into an associated sense that one can never "do enough," so that the belief in one's individual lack turns quickly into guilt:

> *Suzie* (age twenty-three): Well I was working at this horrible job one summer and I just felt like I'm becoming a horrible person because I'm not doing anything for people, right? School was over. I was disconnected with, you know, going out every Thursday to a different activist event. And I just became really, like, oh no. I'm not doing enough.
>
> *Minna*: And when it's really hard to not feel the weight of things, and all things bad when you come into consciousness, it's like, symptomatic white guilt, it's like, whatever. Um, which I dealt with already (laughter), but I do feel like it's hard to say no when you're able to see what is going on and see that you can do something that can contribute to making change.
>
> *Carolyn*: Well I came here [to university] to study music—classical music and—which is something I've done since I was 5. So I don't really remember my life before I ended up being a musician. But got here and you know been having doubts before I came here about going into music. You know had suddenly been exposed to the rest of the world and didn't know if playing in an orchestra was really what I wanted to do or you know feeling a lot of guilt as well for being a musician when all of this other stuff was going on in the world.

One consequence, then, of an individualizing rhetoric about one's own personal responsibility to "save the world" is the psychic cost that comes with carrying a burden too heavy for any one individual to reasonably take on. Such a psychic cost often comes with an associated physical cost; there are many notes from my fieldwork of participants arriving at events or interviews battling colds, being underslept, or nursing some other kind of illness. Also, while this was not a specific question within the interviews, many participants referenced experiences of stress, depression, and burnout.

Gendered Neoliberal Subjects

It is no coincidence that the majority of the excerpts presented earlier are from female participants; such feelings of guilt were more commonly expressed among women than men within my research. There are two ways in which to understand this. The first is to consider the gendered histories of the liberal state, where women are charged with the burden of "caring" as one way in which they can express their citizenship obligations (Arnot & Dillabough 1999; Lister 2003). The second is to appreciate the new pressures that young women face within neoliberal cultural spaces, where "can-do" girls are pitted against their "at-risk" peers (Harris 2004). According to Anita Harris (2004), the twenty-first century "can-do" girl is the new model for engaged citizenship, leading the way in "participating in local communities, and forging harmonious intercultural relationships" (71). Just like the young women represented in the activism article in *Jane* magazine with which this book opened, women are increasingly expected to be the new success stories within neoliberal economies, constantly reconfiguring themselves to meet the demands of a rapidly evolving global economy (Harris 2004; see also Walkerdine et al. 2001).

Given such pressures, it is perhaps not surprising that the women in this study were also the ones to comment upon the struggle between "being happy" and "doing the work." This theme emerged with particular strength within the focus groups where participants had a chance to speak to one another. An extensive discussion ensued during one focus group in which the participants commiserated over the impossibility of "finding balance" while being an activist. The pressure to "be a martyr," as noted by one woman during this discussion, is intense:

> *Diane* (age twenty-two): So I used to feel a lot of stress and tension around [being a] blind purist…One of my triggers are people that are like "if I kill myself the world will be changed." Because that just drives me mental for lots of reasons…it's actually about finding a balance and so still being in the streets—but also not beating myself up every time that I need to buy something that isn't local or organic or whatever labels you want to put on it. Union-made or whatever.

The pressures upon the liberal subject navigating a cultural realm that lays the overwhelming burden for social change on the shoulders of the individual are intense, as described by Diane, so intense that they can push young people to opt out of activist work. In another focus group, one participant who had become actively involved in social justice causes as a young teenager relayed that she had ultimately given up activism because of the associated emotional burdens:

> *Sherry* (age twenty): Yeah, it could have been an age thing and also like sitting in meetings is not fun. I don't enjoy it at all. I don't enjoy emails, I don't enjoy phone calls and I really don't even enjoy rallies. And I enjoy snowboarding and wave boarding and forests and mountains and anyway other people don't [worry about this stuff] (laughing). My mom has been working in activist [groups] for however long in her working life and she's working sometimes 14 hours a day. And it's giving her health problems and she's the most strapping person I've ever met. And she's doing a really good thing, fighting child poverty and putting it on the agenda with this government and stuff like this—really important but her quality of life is terrible. In my opinion. And so I really respect her commitment, [but] I would much rather enjoy my life as much as I can. And smile at everybody and not [feel] angry and disconnected. When I was working in Vancouver activist groups I'd be so angry at the world and everything and I'd go home and I'd cry. I didn't know what to do with myself but it was just so much better having friends and going out and having a really good time.

Sherry here describes in great detail the emotional and physical costs that her involvement in activist work required of her, and her ultimate decision to leave in order to escape these pressures. In the next breath, however, she highlights the guilt that she carries for having abdicated her role as a "good activist" (and good citizen):

> *Sherry*: I mean I realize there's terrible things going on in the world and it's—I feel a little bit selfish to be ignoring all that and just focusing on my own personal happiness. But I do feel that it's one thing that will make the world a better place is more happy people. Instead of one that's just people on their computers.

The dichotomy between "caring for self" and "caring for others" continues to be a burden carried disproportionately by women, judging from the interviews and focus group discussions of this study. Men rarely seemed to find this struggle as pressing (or at least they did not seem to think it important enough to raise as an issue during the research process). Such a struggle perhaps manifests more strongly for women as they balance on the transition point between the liberal and the neoliberal state. Women have historically been positioned under liberalism as the nurturing mother-figures who are meant to find purpose through their caring for others, generally within the private sphere that has been substantially devalued within liberal democracies (Coole 1993; Phillips 1993). Now, as emergent neoliberal subjects *extraordinaire* (Walkerdine et al. 2001), women are expected to "care for themselves"—or, in other words, focus on themselves so as not to expect care from the state. It is perhaps no coincidence that the "good activist" represented on the opening pages of this book comes from a young women's magazine: women have become the new exemplar "good citizen activists" of the neoliberal state.

Not that such a position is an enviable one, nor is it one desired by the women in this study. The pressures upon the neoliberal citizen-activist come at an immense emotional cost, not least because these young women are well aware of the ravages of neoliberalism and the inequality it has generated. This discussion came from the Vancouver focus group:

> *Angela*: I guess I just think that a lot of the drive that is required to sustain activism—doesn't necessarily come from happiness.
> *Minna*: Yeah.
> *Jackie*: Where do you think it comes from?
> *Angela*: (laughing) well it depends on the person. For me—anger or—sadness. For sure.
> *Minna*: And guilt. And privilege can have a lot to do with it too. And also feeling like you have some control over some little slice of your world. Cause if you're not doing anything, you're not, you know, you're doing something with some control. If it's not it feels like you have some control.

The *structures of feeling* that these passages reveal are marked by a flurry of emotions—guilt, anxiety, feeling out of control, sadness, and anger. As women continue to be expected to manage the emotional work associated with social change (Walkerdine & Lucey 1989), they nonetheless seek to find what Minna identifies as "some sense of control"—a sense that they are making their own choices and, in doing so, making a difference for the social issues with which they passionately identify. Ironically, the very belief in the possibility of "making choices" is one of the symptoms of neoliberal subjectivity—that is, the neoliberal subject is forever positioned as a *choosing* subject and thus, for thoughtful and engaged young people, is forever burdened with the fear that one may make the *wrong* choice. Neoliberal discourses constantly undermine any sense of the structuring nature of social life, which means that activists become caught within a paradigm where the path that they and their peers follow appears to them as the result of individual choices that have been individually made. That this is not the case is practically impossible to see from within the subculture itself.

State Histories and Cultural Variations on the Neoliberal Subject

Particularly noteworthy was that emotional responses such as guilt and depression were remarked upon again and again by young people who were born and raised in Canada. By contrast, those young people who had either spent their formative years outside of Western liberal democracies, or had otherwise come to activism through a sense of personal impact, expressed a different array of emotions associated with their activist work. Fernando (age twenty-three) grew up in Latin America and came to Canada as a refugee with his family, escaping political persecution. Judging from his transcripts and my field observations, his approach to activism was much less guilt-ridden. For example, while he sees the value in organizing, he is also interested in partying, dancing, and playing video games, and joked with me in the interview about Canadian activists taking themselves so seriously. Stuart (age twenty-three), who is a member of a First Nations band, also spoke of activism without the inflections of guilt and responsibility that marked many of the other interviews, but rather as a set of opportunities that brought him deeper into his community and allowed him to work on issues that personally affected him. Samina (age twenty-five), who had migrated to the United States and then Canada from India, noted her discomfort with the term "activist," because her activism has arisen out of personal experiences and thus looks very different from that of the wider "activist community" in Canada:

> *Samina*: That's why I don't know if it's really helpful, because I don't really identify as an activist, I don't think I make really conscious decisions. Like around immigration stuff, it's being personally implicated, I've had deportation orders, I've had CSIS [The Canadian Security and Intelligence Service] at my house, I've been detained. It's just kind of how it goes. It's not really an option.

Coded within these different perceptions of activism is the specifically Canadian construction of the good citizen-activist as someone who is working *for and on behalf of others*. Similar to the professed desire to "save the world," this construction of activism situates young activists outside of the issues for which they work, thus reinforcing an individualized as opposed to a communitarian approach to social change. Certainly, there are many within activist communities who have recognized this dichotomy. For example, Spirodon (age twenty-five), a participant who was born and raised in Canada, noted that the fact that people are not personally implicated makes it impossible to develop a genuine social movement, as it will always simply be individuals acting on behalf of others rather than acting for themselves. During the Toronto focus group, an extensive conversation ensued about the fact that activists in the city were often not personally implicated in the causes they fought for, and what this meant. It was agreed during this discussion that the fact that an activist can "choose" to act on a particular issue or not, because he or she is not personally implicated, established an uncomfortable relationship between white middle class activists and the communities with which they worked (which often consisted of racialized people living in poverty).³

How people related to the word "activist" during interviews also speaks volumes about the contradictory claims that are attached to this very controversial term. Some would remark upon their uneasiness about whether they were "entitled" to call themselves activists, wondering whether they had done enough to deserve the name. Others disliked the term and preferred not to use it, choosing "organizer" or "agitator" over "activist," which they felt had been co-opted. This array of responses to the notion of "the activist" is mirrored within broader cultural scripts. The controversy about what makes an "activist" in fact highlights many of the competing strands with which this book is concerned. We have on the one hand "the activist" as good citizen, the active, engaged individual who also happens to carry a number of middle-class markers (cf. Craig Kielburger, or the women in *Jane* magazine). This "activist" is the true heir to liberal democratic values and its incipient child, neoliberalism. The "activist," in this case, is motivated by feelings of individual responsibility to the state and community (which turn quickly to feelings of guilt if one's perceived responsibility is not fulfilled), and ultimately curtails his or her behavior so as to not challenge the state beyond particular limits. It also takes place within an individualized frame that assumes a rational actor making individual decisions separate from any sense of integrated relationships, and using activism as one aspect of a larger project of perpetual self-improvement. It is this notion of activism that participants are implicitly referencing when they want to distance themselves from the term as a state-sanctioned and placated version of the work they are attempting to do.

On the other hand, there lies "the activist" as enemy of the state, the troublemaking hooligans who are to be found on the front covers of newspapers being dragged away by heavily armored police. These representations of "the activist" carry their own peculiar weight within activist subcultures, whereby one is seen as "more committed" if one has been identified by the state as a troublemaker. These are, perhaps, the images that come to mind when people are not certain they deserve the label "activist." Thus the peculiar legacies of liberalism and neoliberalism, class codes of accomplishment, histories of racialized exclusions, and the gendered subject within the neoliberal state create a particular cultural space within which young people experience, emotionally and bodily, the demands and requirements of activist cultures.

Policing the Neoliberal Subject

The idea of the good citizen in neoliberal times carries more bodily implications for young activists navigating the contemporary nation-state.[4] Beyond inculcating self-regulating ideas about morality and guilt, the idea of the good young citizen appears to be playing a role in activists' interactions with police. Many young activists within this study had experienced brutal treatment at the hands of the Canadian police (municipal, provincial, and federal), particularly in the post-9/11 era, where it appears that police repression of dissent has become more acceptable in the face of public anxiety about "terrorist threats." Aggressive policing can be understood as a neoliberal practice linked to governance (see Brown 2005), designed to create anxiety and guilt. It does so, in part, by targeting those who are seen to have overstepped the bounds of legitimate citizenship behavior—as delimited through and operating within such sites as education and media. Thus policing acts not only as a powerful material force limiting certain kinds of activist expression, it also serves as a state-sanctioned symbolic marker of the (ever-shrinking) limits to democratic participation for young people.

Policing was often experienced as a pervasive presence that shaped multiple modalities of activist interaction, including the specific forms that a protest could take. Discourses of the good or legitimate citizen were often immanent in these accounts, held up as a model for appropriate "freedom of speech" protest that did not, however, cross the line into "rabble-rousing" activism.

> *Carolyn*: I wasn't in [the anti-FTAA protests in] Quebec City, I wasn't in [the anti-WTO protests in] Seattle. I wasn't in any of those big protests. And everything I've done—*it's not that it's been tame* but it's been done in coordination with the police

you know. The big rally that happened last year on December 3rd for the UN conference was in coordination with the police. You know, you get your permits. You did it all according to the law. When we did all our media stunts, you know the police were there but we had our permits and we had sorted all of it out and it was very amicable and stuff. (Emphasis mine)

Carolyn's description carries signifiers of the cultural subtext that accompanies Canadian youth activism, and the relationship it has to policing. For example, in describing her activism, she feels compelled to note that "it's not that it's been tame," or in other words, it's not that it's been ineffective, within the paradigm of activist engagement. She is responding to an internal struggle within activist circles about appropriate police involvement, and what this means for activist effectiveness, as captured by Rajinder in the following extract:

Rajinder: I was in Montreal and I was in this one demonstration...And it was really wonderful. Like, I felt it was really empowering. But then there are those demonstrations that are not...How can you leave a rally down? Like feeling less hopeful. You should leave a rally empowered and ready to start another one the next day. Ready to start getting involved. But there are those rallies where you just go to them and it's very much just marching down the street. And there's no power to it...But then some people would say, oh, you know, we can't be confrontational with the police and demonstrations nowadays...that's counter-productive. But then, at the same time, when we want a desired effect and when there's so much anger and resentment, should we comply with what they want and have this kind of model, nice, sweet demo where there's, you know, the police smiling and the activists smiling and then, they do their little march with no kind of direct confrontation and you have speeches. So there is definitely something wrong when you leave a march feeling disempowered...Like, when these demonstrations are presented as oh...look at us, we're a democratic society. These are people exerting their democratic right.

Whether the police have been invited to a rally by organizers or not, their presence plays a particular role that functions beyond the mere enforcement of law. Rather, they serve as a symbolic and material reminder of the limits of acceptable citizenship behavior—as Rajinder notes, the rallies reinforce the notion of Canada as a democratic society, while simultaneously the police presence prevents such "democratic" behavior from erupting into something that might pose a more fundamental challenge to injustices. The police neither need to threaten force, nor use tear gas or rubber bullets to serve as a restraining force on youth behavior. The very possibility of arrest can be sufficient for young people to self-regulate, as good neoliberal citizens ought, so as to avoid the potential repercussions that accrue from carrying a criminal record.

If, on the other hand, young people refuse to follow the state-imposed strictures attached to the good citizen, the repercussions can be severe. From Farah:

> *Farah*: There was just like a disperse order [from the police] and no one was leaving in any rush. And a bunch of people had been arrested. So we decided we were going to walk down to the jail, so we started another march away from the Sheraton, which was where [the protest] was. And all of a sudden cops just started charging from everywhere—riot cops just on foot. And lots of cops on horses. And this guy couldn't see and the cops were coming from everywhere because we'd been tear gassed so badly and [so] I stopped to help him and I was holding onto both my friends' hands and I let go and somehow this guy got away and all of a sudden I was like on the ground and they had like six cops on me and they were just wailing away on me. Um, and that was kind of a chain reaction like one friend stopped and then got arrested. And then another one stopped cause they stopped and we ended up all getting arrested.

Farah's encounter with the police, among other factors in her life, led to posttraumatic stress disorder so severe that her hair fell out and she became chronically depressed. She describes another encounter she had with the police:

> *Farah*: [The police] did massive roundups a couple of years in a row. That was really brutal. It was freezing rain in winter. And they kept us outside like squished together surrounded by cops in full riot gear for 4 hours or something in the rain. It was

awful. People were peeing and like yeah. And they kept us on buses handcuffed really badly for a long time. And then I was racially harassed by one of the cops during that whole altercation. They—when they were booking me or whatever—they were tossing me around, calling me Islam. They kept referring to me as Islam—my last name is Islamic so.

Both Farah's experiences and her account connect to a longer history of who is deemed "acceptable" within the nation-state, as documented within the "detour" of chapter two. Her description of the police treatment of the activists—massive roundups, being squished together, people forced to urinate in close quarters—evokes an image of activists as less-than-human, as beings without rights within the liberal democratic state (Arendt 1998; Benhabib 2004). Farah's specific experience of racial harassment is similarly tied to a particular history of the legitimate citizen—as we saw in the previous chapter, this category within Canada has until recently been limited to white people (Abu-Laban 1998). Thus we can understand the practices of policing to be predicated upon, at least in part, histories of the "legitimate citizen" that, through their actions, police are attempting to strip from activists. This is a powerful warning indeed to young people who have ventured past the limits of acceptable citizenship behavior.

Kieran also had several encounters with the police. After being arrested during the anti-FTAA (Free Trade Area of the Americas) protests in Quebec City, as part of a "roundup" similar to the one described by Farah, he was ultimately told that his charges had been dropped. Five years later, he was organizing a major march in Montreal and learned that was not the case.

> *Kieran*: [The police] called me up the night before the march and said...we have a warrant for your arrest, we have a bench warrant and we have to exercise it and we have 20 officers looking for you...
>
> *Jackie*: Wow. So last year you're getting ready to organize a big protest march. Or a big march.
>
> *Kieran*: *March. Not a protest...A march in support of action on climate change...*The day before, the night before, I was on my way to a social, which I'd organized for all the youth at the climate negotiations...And then I got a call...it was this

police officer. I mean, in retrospect I wish I'd never taken it...And he said, oh we have this warrant for your arrest and I said you've got to be joking me, like, you know, you had five years. You had my number, you had my address, da, da, da. What the hell? Well, that doesn't matter now. I want you to come meet me. I was like, I'm not going to come meet you somewhere...So I basically said well I'll call you back when I've spoken to my lawyer because I don't need to talk to you at all until I speak to my lawyer...Anyway, I went into hiding. Pretty much went into hiding with the march coordinator. And we spent the night, called all the unions and then got a union lawyer...And anyway we spent the morning on the phones working it out and then finally got the police to agree not to arrest me at the march. So I went to the march and the march was great. (Emphasis mine)

Although it is possible that the timing of the renewed police interest in Kieran's case and his organizing of a large-scale march were coincidental, Kieran and his legal advisors certainly felt that it was more than that. Kieran drew on broader discourses of citizen legitimacy by emphasizing that he was organizing a "march" over a "protest" (the former being something that good citizens do, the latter being the action of a bad activist). This semantic tactic may well have worked in his favor as he and his lawyers negotiated with the police for him to be allowed to complete his work—that is, a march in support of combating climate change, easily aligned with the contemporary notion of the "good citizen" in early twenty-first century Canada.

Conclusions

The production and regulation of the "good citizen" within the Canadian state is accomplished through a variety of cultural means, not least of which emanate from schooling but which also extend beyond its boundaries. The possibility for active participation within the state, while explicated as an ideal of the new civics curricula, comes with a particular set of limits and expectations about what such participation looks like. Drawing on histories of liberalism and current ideologies of neoliberalism, the "active citizen" idealized through schooling and media is one who engages with the state through self-regulated acts of "responsible" citizenship that are limited to individual encounters with the electoral process, charitable community work, and participation through formal aspects of the political system, such as official parties. Aside from being almost entirely meaningless within the context of young people's lives, these forms of citizenship participation replicate the idea of democracy as being something that takes place only through liberal democratic structures—that is, only through the individual's relation to the state, as an individual. Critiques of this particular vision for democracy are widespread and long-standing (see Arendt 1998; Brown 1995, 2001; Habermas 1996; Hernández 1997; Mouffe 1993; I. M. Young 1990 for a few examples).

What is of particular interest in this phenomenon is how cultural messages about the "good citizen" are employed, refuted, and responded to within youth activist subcultures themselves. What does it mean to engage in activism as a young person within the current configurations of contradictory messages? On the one hand, the message from civics curricula and the Craig Kielburgers of the world is that one's citizenship duty includes acts of charity that are often relabeled as "activism"—so activism is good. On the other hand, those who engage in forms of activism that directly confront the state and its policies are represented as maniacs—so activism is bad. Weaving through this are the immanent cultural messages about the (neo)liberal subject and his or her responsibility to the state (whereby failure is then converted to guilt), as well as the classed, gendered, and racialized aspects of citizenship and belonging, such that the particular cultural space through which young activists must pass is a quagmire of contradictory messages and implications. How have youth activist subcultures responded to this particular cultural sphere? I move forward to address this question in the next chapter.

4

Class Exclusions, Racialized Identities: The Symbolic Economy of Youth Activism

> Cultures are good for many things: good to communicate with, good to find identity through, good for establishing mutuality and reciprocity. They are good for all these, and more perhaps, because at bottom, they are also good for "thinking with."
> —Willis 2000, 35

Thus far, this book has traced the development of the young activist-citizen through a focus on the macrostructures that contribute to the cultural sphere: state institutions such as education, media representations, ideological influences of liberalism and neoliberalism, and the historical moments that shape the textures of the present. This chapter turns now to the micro-sociological elements of a culture, the aspects of culture that Paul Willis identifies as "good for thinking with." It is within this chapter that many of the theoretical tools from cultural sociological approaches, such as that of Pierre Bourdieu and others influenced by his work, come to the forefront. The chapter thus begins with an overview of the relevant concepts that shape the analysis to follow. It then goes on to trace the influences of factors such as family history, class, and "race" on the constitution of youth activist subcultures. The fundamental aim of the chapter is to draw explicit lines of connection between the macrostructures that have been the focus of the first half of the book, and the everyday symbolic economy of youth activist cultures themselves. In doing so, I hope to illuminate the essential interconnections between the macro and the micro, in order to gain a more complex grasp of the complicated context within which Citizen Youth currently resides.

Theorizing Youth Activist Subcultures: Symbolic Economies, Habitus and Subcultural Capital

Members of a subculture often understand the "symbolic economy" of their own subcultural group at an almost unconscious level. The term "economy" implies a form of exchange; as Skeggs (2004) notes, "counting is not what is important in understanding exchange, but rather *the relationships* that enable exchange to take place" (10; emphasis in the original). It is within these relationships that the symbolic economy of activism finds its meaning, where formations of class and "race" are "dynamic, produced through conflict and fought out at the level of the symbolic" (5). Like that of Skeggs, my analysis is grounded within Bourdieu's (1997) concept of "symbolic capital": "One of the most unequal of all distributions, and probably, in any case, the most cruel, is the distribution of symbolic capital, that is, of social importance and of reasons for living" (241). Julie Bettie (2003) uses the concept "symbolic economy" in a similar manner within her ethnography of working class girls in rural California. In Bettie's field site, "[h]airstyles, clothes, shoes, and the colors of lipstick, lip liner, and nail polish" were essential elements "employed to express group membership as the body became a resource and a site on which difference was inscribed" (62). Similarly, this chapter explores the manner in which elements such as style, comportment, political beliefs, and language are used by youth activists to signal their belonging within the subcultural group. Located within a cultural context that has been stratified by class and "race" since Canada's inception as a nation-state, it is perhaps not surprising that the symbolic economy of youth activist subcultures is similarly marked by class and "race" exclusions.

This chapter is largely framed within Pierre Bourdieu's cultural sociological perspective on social relations and inequality. Bourdieu suggests that every *field* contains a *doxa*, whereby a field can be broadly understood as the specific sociocultural context within which people interact, and the doxa of the field encapsulates the set of common-sense assumptions that are inherent to that field. A field, which Bourdieu also calls the "social space," works on the bodies that inhabit it so that, if they are able, individuals begin to align themselves with the appropriate doxa so as to feel "at ease" within the social space:

> The structures of the social space (or of fields) shape bodies by inculcating in them, through the conditionings associated with a position in that space, the cognitive structures that these conditionings apply to them. More precisely, the social world, because it is an object of knowledge for those who are included in it, is, in part, the reified or incorporated product of all the different (and rival) acts of knowledge of which it is the object. (Bourdieu 1997, 183)

He describes the "cognitive structures" required to navigate the social space (or field) as a form of *practical knowledge* that emerges psychically and bodily within or between the players in the field. That is, the people who make up the social space each embody a sense of what it means to belong to a particular space, and what the relational rules are that will dictate one's belonging or exclusion within the space. He writes:

> Each agent has a practical, bodily knowledge of her present and potential position in the social space, a "sense of one's place," as Goffmann puts it, converted into a *sense of placement* which governs her experience of the place occupied,... defined absolutely and above all relationally as a rank, and the way to behave in order to keep it ("pulling rank") and to keep within it ("knowing one's place," etc). (184; emphasis in the original)

The relation of *habitus* to field is a complex one; Bourdieu describes the habitus as "a system of dispositions to be and to do, [it] is a potentiality, a desire to be which, in a certain way, seeks to create the conditions of its fulfillment, and therefore to create the conditions most favorable to what it is" (150). He sees the process by which the agent seeks out a field most compatible with his or her own habitus as taking place through the practical implementation of such emotional responses to situations as "sympathies and antipathies, affections and aversions, tastes and distastes" (150). It is these emotional responses that assist an individual in determining whether he or she feels "at home" in the social space and through which one can fulfill "one's desire to be which one identifies with happiness" (ibid.).

It is within the specific social space or field that one's *cultural capital* becomes relevant—that is, cultural capital is not a universal attribute that can be accommodated across all fields. This idea is best captured, particularly in the case of youth subcultures, by Sarah Thornton's (1996) notion of *subcultural capital*, which highlights the inextricably contextual nature of cultural capital. Thornton describes subcultural capital as "embodied in the form of being 'in-the-know'" (11), a process of identification and recognition that is highly context-dependent. Such capital must still be subjected to a class analysis, whereby one's capacity to take up and enact a specific subcultural identity is shaped by one's class position within a stratified society. The harms that such stratification can engender for individuals within the social space is further captured by Bourdieu's concept of "symbolic violence." Where cultural capital can be understood most simply as "the investment of economic resources in cultural assets and embodied social attributes and propensities" (Moore 2004, 446), Bourdieu's typology is made more complex by noting that it is the nature of cultural capital to be *systematically misrecognized*. This misrecognition serves to obscure the ways in which it is initially linked to economic status (Moore 2004). It is through this obfuscation that the enactment of cultural capital within a specific field comes to be linked to forms of power, and how it can thus become an integral aspect of the symbolic violence that helps to maintain the distinctions between those who feel that they are "in place" (or "in the know") versus those who are "out of place."

The manner in which cultural capital plays out within fields that are outside of the mainstream—within subcultures, in other words—becomes further complicated by the relation of what Cohen (1997) has referred to as a "dominated culture" to a "dominant" one. Within youth activist subcultures, it is often clear that people have sought each other out as a form of refuge against a wider mainstream culture that many find to be intensely problematic. This does not mean, however, that they are able to escape the larger relations of power within which we are all embedded in a stratified society. However, I would suggest, *because of their very existence as a subculture*, the forms of symbolic violence become more difficult to discern, as the potential for misrecognition increases the farther the group positions itself from the mainstream. In particular, when a subculture is explicitly concerned with issues of economic and social inequality (such as is the case with youth activism), the manner in which its members reproduce aspects of these very inequalities become particularly mystified. One way in which this happens is through the enactment of what Julie Bettie (2003) calls "class performances." Bettie coined the term "class performance" to highlight the ways in which one's class of origin does not always neatly coincide with the class location that one represents to the world. She thus makes an important connection to the *cultural enactment* of class, noting that while such cultural performances are most often linked to one's habitus (and thus one's unconscious enactment of class), the possibility of a "class performance" explains what happens when one's class enactment is not directly mappable onto one's habitus (cf. 51). Bettie's concept of "class performances" begins to nuance Thornton's subcultural capital in that it permits the possibility of enacting a class behavior that does not match one's class origins, without losing sight of the delimiting nature of class histories.

What forms, then, of subcultural capital are most desirable within youth activist communities? Within the span of my fieldwork, I came to understand the predominant type of class performance that accrues the most subcultural capital within youth activist communities as a complex form of *working class/middle class performance*, or what I have called more simply "*performing grunge*." This performance has attained a specific cultural code also known as being "radical." While such a performance is certainly neither ubiquitous nor entirely determining of who becomes involved in these communities, the idea of being "radical" emerged so often in interviews and field work that I think it can best be understood as a specific cultural script, the articulation of which points to some hidden (or not-so-hidden) class harms experienced by a number of research participants. Although this performance generally emerged along class lines, it had specific implications for those participants who were from racialized communities as well. This was due, in part, to the inextricable relationship between class and "race" within Canada, and also due to the fact of the normative (read: white) Canadian citizen against which all young people are expected to measure themselves.

Developing an Activist Habitus: Families of Origin

The vast majority of participants within this research project were raised by middle-class families.[1] This middle-class history was moderated by another important factor in the context of the research; that is, participants were remarkable for being largely from left-leaning,[2] if not outright activist, families. Of the thirty-three participants for whom I have data,[3] fifteen identified that their parents were either activists themselves, or highly engaged in lefty political practices (e.g., campaigned for the politically left-leaning New Democratic Party). Another twelve identified their parents as supportive of their activist work, and generally in agreement with their left-leaning views, even if they were not themselves actively engaged in organizing. Three saw their parents as supportive of their activist work, even though they did not share the same political values. Only three remarked that their parents were entirely unsupportive of their activist work, largely because their political values were in conflict with those of their children.

In keeping with Bourdieu's concept of the *habitus*, the implications for young people coming from middle-class activist and/or lefty families was that they had first-hand experience of the largely middle-class *field* of activism. Many spoke of attending their first protest when they were children, on the shoulders of parents who were demonstrating against nuclear facilities, the first Iraq War, or other social issues of their generation. This played an important role in the activism of those people whose parents were so involved. As Zoe (age twenty-two) remarked about the influence of her parents' activism on her own political practices:

> *Zoe*: Oh hugely, because I think it endowed me with an ability to talk about politics, and an interest in talking about politics. More than just politics, because of all the connotations of that, is like a sense of justice. My dad and my mum both have a really deep sense of justice. Whether I agree with it all the time or not, but my dad was actually the only man still that I have ever met that was so sensitive about war that he would freely cry talking about war any time. So yeah, that was really powerful for me as a kid.

Likewise, Carolyn (age twenty) noted the following about her family:

> *Carolyn*: Everyone's really socially involved so it's an interesting dynamic to come from 'cause in some ways it feels like there's so much support behind it. In some ways it kind of feels like I'm the last one that's coming along you know... [I] couldn't be anything but an activist. It's just sort of expected. You know it's a phenomenal family to grow up in.

Returning to Bourdieu's notion of the habitus, and the role it plays in structuring people's process of seeking out a field that matches their own sensibilities and experiences, we can begin to see how the experience of growing up in a home that explicitly focused on social justice concerns could both predispose a person to seek out such social spaces, as well as provide them with the dispositions that would make accommodation within these spaces a relatively straightforward task. Such homes almost exclusively belonged to participants who were both white and middle class, structuring the forms of access that could be negotiated to the activist habitus that made a sense of belonging within the activist field more easily attainable. Particularly noteworthy was that those who came from activist families were much more likely to be involved at a younger age, and to have achieved leadership positions within activist groups.

I had the opportunity to observe a snippet of the early socialization process that could contribute to the development of such a habitus, a process that may have been similar to that experienced by some of the participants in this research. While I was in the middle of an interview at the home of Diana (age twenty-two), we were interrupted by her roommate's four-year-old daughter, who was trying to avoid going to daycare. She came into the living room where we were seated carrying a doll with her, a sort of Barbie doll fairy, in order to show it to us. While admiring the toy, Diana asked the child, Jillian, if she remembered what they had been speaking of about this particular toy earlier: "There was some reason we don't like this dolly, right?" Diana asked her. Jillian looked up at us sideways, toy clutched in one hand. "Yes...," she said hesitantly, "because it's Disney." "And why don't we like Disney?" Diana asked her. Jillian shook her head, looking perplexed. "Because they use child labor, remember?" Diana prompted her. Jillian continued to look confused: "What's child labor?" she asked. At this point her harried mom, also an activist, came down the stairs calling for Jillian to get her boots on and get on the road to daycare. "Ask your mom on your way to daycare," Diana urged her. As Jillian and her mom left the room, we heard Jillian ask, "Mommy, what's child labor?" (field notes, October 27, 2006).

Such experiences do not, of course, capture all of the childhoods of the participants in this project. Participants whose families may have been broadly supportive but were not, themselves, activists or left-leaning found themselves needing to negotiate the "lack-of-fit" that existed between their habitus and the field of activism. Conrad (age twenty-five), who came from an Indo-Canadian family without a history of Canadian activism, relates an amusing story that poignantly illustrates the difference in habitus acquired by him and his siblings to that which Jillian is being exposed to:

> *Conrad*: My younger brothers and sisters, like they're all kind of aware of it, but again, like they challenge it in kind of funny ways. Like my brother went to England, and he got me like this Che Guevara t-shirt, right? Cause I always liked Rage Against the Machine, and Rage Against the Machine always had this stuff. And then, he got me like a bottle of rum another time, and I was like it's Che rum, I was like, ok, this is totally against what he stands for, right? But that's my brother giving me a

gift, right? And then like a couple of years later, my sister got me for my birthday a Che Guevara t-shirt, and I was like, you guys don't really understand. But then that's my brother and sister, they're going to be supportive of it in some ways. And my mom and dad, though, they're just like whatever, right? There's, in the Indo-Canadian community, even in our family, there's an understanding of the importance of politics, of democracy, and things like that, but it's always an understanding of it at the party level, right? There's an awareness of NDP, Liberal, what are you, I'm not Liberal, but in terms of political philosophy and believing any of that stuff, not really.

Conrad's experience, as relayed here, helps to illustrate the complex and deeply symbolic ways in which one's family background can contribute to a sense of belonging—or exclusion— within activist life worlds. He describes his family's attempts to support what they thought of as his interest, without a deeper appreciation for the nuances of appropriate activist behavior. Hence, the gift of Che Guevara paraphernalia, offered as a token of affection, in fact contravened unspoken activist rules about permissible gear and attire. The Che image to which Conrad is referring, known as the Guerrillero Heroico, has been identified as both an activist icon representing the "resolve to fight injustice and free the world from cruelty and injustice" and an image that has been exploited as "designer revolutionary-ism for trendy popular consumption" (Cambre 2009, 339; see also Heath and Potter 2004). As such, it is a complex piece of activist iconography that requires careful handling in order to mark one as "in the know" within the symbolic economy of youth activist cultures—a distinction that Conrad obviously feels his siblings do not quite understand. That such an activist habitus was almost exclusively affiliated with a specific class history (i.e., middle class) meant that only some young people could access the subcultural community of youth activism via this route; in other words, this particular modality of acquiring an activist habitus through family histories of middle class activism was a very specific and delimited route. When combined with the general cultural sanction against taking up forms of citizenship that challenge the state—such as the activities of many of the activists within this project—the structuring nature of the class-based activist habitus effectively constrains *who* might take up the political location of the "activist."

"Race" and the Activist Habitus

Conrad's story highlights another complicating aspect of youth activist identity within the contemporary Canadian nation-state: that is, the role of "race" or ethnicity. Just as in many aspects of Canadian society, the existence of racism within activist circles is a hotly debated topic. Specifically, there have been many articles, conversations, and Internet discussions about whether activist communities are racist (see, e.g., Numerous authors 2003). While these debates have been important ones, and the issues they raise continue to require attention, they tend to overlook one of the key intersecting factors that complicate the issue of racism within activist cultures. Specifically, it can be difficult to extricate class from "race," particularly in a country such as Canada with its legacies of colonialism and racist migration policies. As noted previously, the idea of the "good citizen" has long been associated with an imaginary of white middle classness. Additionally, middle-class cultures that can easily accommodate an activist habitus remain largely white. When this is combined with the specific opportunity structures that are available to people from ethnic minority communities, particularly if they are recent immigrants, it becomes less easy to access the forms of subcultural knowledge required to navigate activist cultures. Within a wider cultural context that consistently devalues and degrades forms of activist practice transgressing the unwritten rules of the "good citizen," it is not always possible for newcomer families to incorporate the social justice habitus that seems to be one of the common precursors to youth activist engagement. Thus, rather than simply indicting them for being "racist," I am trying to make the more complex argument that activist cultures within Canada, which come from a specific history of white middle-classness (see Levitt 1984; Palmer 2009), unintentionally reproduce subcultural practices that serve to exclude people who have not been exposed to the "common sense" values of that white, middle-class structure of feeling about activism. The result is that although many visible minority young people find their way into activist cultures, many of them also experience the sense of "not quite fitting," which means their interactions within activist cultures are often somewhat uneasy.[4]

Noteworthy here is that the "whiteness" of activist cultures was often commented upon by both white activists and activists of color, while its middle-classness went largely unremarked. For example, Diane, a white participant, relayed a joke to me: "Question: How do you know if you're an anarchist? Answer: All your clothes are black and all your friends are white." There are some obvious reasons for the fact that class remained invisible while "race" and racism were more easily observed. First of all, "whiteness" appears to be more evident than "middle-classness," especially with the prevalence of working-class performances—what I have called "performing grunge"—within activist cultures (described further later). But there is another way in which class has become invisible, unique to places such as Canada and the United States with their rhetoric of meritocracy and liberal equality: that is, class and "race" have come to be conflated in ways that render class invisible. Bettie (2003) noted that working-class girls within the rural California high school where she carried out her fieldwork often denied their class location as a way to protect themselves against class harms and in response to feelings of shame. In many ways, "race" has become the new class, standing in for concerns about equity and access to resources. The problem here is that it can never be "race" alone as a singular category that structures such access, although it certainly plays a powerful role in a white-dominant country such as Canada. But when "race" signifies inequality as the superordinate category it can serve to obscure the important role of class in structuring youth activist subcultures.

Just as was true for white participants, almost all of the participants of color that I interviewed came from middle- or upper middle-class histories. While constantly facing the wider politics of "race" in urban Canada, I would suggest that their class markers provided them, to a certain degree, with the forms of cultural capital that permitted them to better navigate youth activist subcultures. Nonetheless their "race"/ethnicity also played an important role in preventing them from feeling as if they quite "fit." I see this as arising from two conditions: first, the long coexistence between "whiteness" and the idea of the "good citizen." Second, the structuring nature of the activist family habitus, and more specifically the way in which visible minority activists often had to navigate between a family culture that did not coincide with the specific habitus of activist cultures, and the subcultural rules of Canadian youth activism.

The first instance became most evident when discussing the idea of citizenship with Aboriginal participants and participants of color.[5] Stuart (age twenty-three) reflects on his own experiences of the racialized exclusions he encountered through schooling:

> *Stuart*: I think in social studies, this message became very obvious to me, how society at large in Canada is set up. I got a distinct impression that there was some false kind of facts fed to us... I just got the impression through these text books that Canada is this great thing, it's like the be all, end all panacea, it will solve all your societal problems, and [yet] there was all these different instances of injustice, where there'd be the Chinese Head Tax, or every other mile there's a dead Chinaman, having the Sikhs and Punjabs sent back to India, the Japanese internment, all these different racially based injustices. It became really obvious to me, they're not giving us the straight facts, this isn't the truth, this is like a euphemized version of his-story.

As a member of a First Nations band, Stuart was also highly critical of his experiences within mainstream schooling: for example, of being "streamed" into classes with lower academic expectations, and being in a class about First Nations culture that focused on what he described derisively as "an arts and crafts kind of class, like making drums, rattles, all these little trinkets."

As demonstrated through the "detour," Canada's history consists of numerous repetitions of the representation of ethnic minority and Aboriginal peoples as being undeserving of citizenship status, constituted through a normative reference to a specific Euro-centric version of "whiteness." Those who cannot lay claim to this form of "normalcy" are forced to reconcile their own bodily realities with what they have learned about Canada's apparently inclusive "citizenship." As Nancy (age twenty), whose family came to Canada from Eritrea, notes, "society will never view me as Canadian." Other participants made similar remarks:

> *Sanna* (age nineteen): But I guess more than anything I'd have to say that I'm Canadian. But there is that, so now becoming more conscious, I've noticed that disparity between, like I can't just say I'm Canadian, but a white person could be like "well, I'm Canadian," and you don't have to be like "no, you're not, because you're not Aboriginal so you're definitely not Canadian." One of the terms that we use in my [university] classes that I think is such a solid term is the notion of being forever hyphenated, and always needing that "Indo-Canadian," you know, "Kenyan-Canadian," needing that hyphen to be legitimized. So I think my connection to citizenship right now is one of increasing uncomfortability.
>
> *Fouzia* (age twenty-four): If people ask me what I am I say I'm Pakistani-Canadian. But that's a very surfacy, almost like "how are you, I'm fine" type of answer. You know? I think the sticky thing with citizenship and with Canada is everything is really glossed over... Before I used to be really fine with considering yourself as Canadian and being almost proud and like I think it's all in context in relation to other things. Like in relation to America? I'm glad I'm in Canada. In relation to the rest of the world? I don't know. But I'm just in Canada. Do I identify as a Canadian? Uh, I don't know. Like I don't really know. I don't know if I'm answering this correctly. (*Laughs*)

These assertions of ambivalence about a Canadian identity stood in sharp contrast to the ease with which white participants could own their Canadian citizenship, even if they felt angry or embarrassed by the historical and current actions of Canada as a nation-state. The need that young people from racialized groups felt to "hyphenate" themselves spoke to deeper emotions of exclusion and belonging. It also highlights the deeply symbolic ways in which national imaginaries, which are fundamentally contingent upon the history of citizenship in Canada, regulate how one thinks about oneself in the context of the state.

Whether or not one feels that one "belongs" to Canada is constituted in large part by the ways in which other people react to one's purported place in the nation. That is, no matter how much one might feel a sense of "belonging" within Canada, if one does not match the cultural imaginary of the proper citizen, then one will continually be reminded that one does not, in fact, belong:

> *Fouzia*: So maybe to me, I think, citizenship equates to actual acceptance or ground-rooted belonging within where you're from or where you live. And I've never had that sense of complete belonging. Ever. Within my experiences, within my childhood, within anything that I've done. I can tell you right from my childhood, you know, we were Muslim. We were living in [a] predominantly white neighbourhood. Things like when Eid would come around, it's an Islamic festival, like Islamic day, Mum would be really wanting to have us energized over this cultural day. So she would put mhendi on our hands. Like, henna. So I remember the next day I went to school and I had henna on my hands and the teacher asked a question. I put up my hand and for the rest of that morning, till the afternoon, I was being taunted about having this disease growing on my hands. And like the principal found me in the washroom bawling my eyes out trying to scrub the henna off my hands.
>
> *Farah* (age twenty-seven): [I] definitely grew up thinking I was an immigrant. You know, like knowing I was an immigrant. And having a father with a weird accent and getting called nigger at elementary school and being told to go back to where I come from, from neighbours and having a weird name and having different birth certificates and all this kind of stuff. You know, that are markers in you feeling different.

These everyday encounters with racism within the cultural field of schooling make up the unofficial curriculum that young people incorporate into their understandings of themselves and their role within the nation-state. They are remarkable for their continuity with histories of "race"-based exclusions, as documented in the "detour." Remarkable also are the ways in which such experiences engender a specific structure of feeling—in this case, of feeling excluded, taunted, and different—and what this means for young people's material relationship to the concept of citizenship. No matter how much loyalty they might feel toward the "imagined community" (Anderson 2006) of the Canadian nation—and many participants remarked that they began schooling with just such a feeling of patriotism—their experiences within the educational system and the broader cultural sphere have left them ambivalent and uncertain, and with a sense that they do not quite belong "here" but neither do they belong anywhere else. From within a liberal democratic state, where one's belonging *to* the state is the basis for legitimation upon which one claims the rights of citizenship (i.e., the right to have rights, see Arendt 1998; Benhabib 2004),[6] the impact of racism within Canadian schools can act to further limit the participation of those from racialized communities within even the narrow range of options offered through schooling as acts of citizenship.

The second manner in which "race" appears to be implicated in youth activist subcultures is through the more general experience for participants of color of being forced to navigate between so-called Canadian norms and those of their own families or wider ethnocultural communities, who often had quite different cultural practices and norms. It is here that the existence of a particular Canadian activist habitus—which was often not shared by the families of participants of color—appeared to be particularly powerful. This experience, as relayed by participants through interviews, often manifested as a need to negotiate between their own ethnocultural communities, including their embedded values and beliefs, and that of activist subcultures, in a manner that sometimes left them feeling that they must pit one against the other. As Sanna noted:

> *Sanna*: I think I connect more with people in a space like [a class on community activism], or you know, a political or organizing space that are around my age, or that are even not my age, than I do in a Muslim context where they're my age. There are definitely things that we connect with, but even though my religion is so important for me, it's harder for me to reconcile political and unpolitical, than Muslim and not Muslim.

Will (age twenty-three) made a similar comment:

> *Will*: I don't feel like I belong to the Markham community [where I grew up], that's for sure... At the same time it's very interesting because it's got a huge minority population. Lots of Chinese in Markham as well as a South Asian population... So. In terms of racial, like ethnic identity I don't even feel connected with the Chinese people in Markham because a lot of them are very new, are very wealthy and don't hold the same values as I do... My Chinese language, it's not there yet. It's not as strong. And it's a weird kind of in-between, right? Because... in terms of a greater identity I find it more easy to relate to the activist circle and the people that I do work with just because values are very important.

This experience of internal conflict and of needing to "choose" between loyalty to family and ethnocultural community or compliance with activist norms and values highlights the "lack of fit" between habitus and field for participants who did not grow up within a white activist family. Although these participants share a similar class location as many of their activist peers—Sanna's father is an imam and her mother is a teacher, and she grew up in a comfortable family home within the suburbs of Vancouver, whereas Will's father is an accountant, and his mother is university-educated and has worked in a variety of middle-class occupations—their families do not share the white activist habitus that would allow Sanna and Will to "belong" within Canadian youth activist subcultures without the possibility of betraying their family of origin. Sanna makes this fear explicit when she states:

> *Sanna*: [It's] been really tough, like trying to convince [them] that it's okay, convince my parents that there is a lot of fluidity to that [activist] identity, and that you can negotiate different circles, and yeah, they're on some level a bit uncomfortable with me getting too involved in thinking that, you know, they're losing me to a society that they're not totally comfortable with.

"Race" further interconnects with class here through a recent history of migration, and the meanings this generates for class experiences and aspirations. Although Will's and Sanna's families had managed to find a place within the opportunity structures of Canada—partially due in each case to significant economic and cultural capital in their respective countries of birth—both families were haunted by the specters of economic failure and social exclusion for their children. Will notes that his parents are not thrilled with his political work, and that they continue to hold out hopes that he will become a doctor—"the Chinese dream," as he calls it. Sanna's parents are worried that she will abandon values or perspectives that they hold dear. Such emotionally fraught negotiations create a significant barrier that is not faced by white participants from middle-class activist families. Although these young activists have so far managed to tread this complex territory, the existence of these tensions force them to continually make difficult choices that could, at any point, lead them away from activism. This could especially be the case if the cost—in the form of lost or strained relations with family or other ethnocultural community members—becomes too high.

Although the examples I have drawn from the stories of Sanna, Will, and Conrad were consistent with the stories of some of the other participants of color, it is important to note that there were exceptions to this experience. These differences reinforce the importance of an intersecting analysis that considers both "race" and class, as well as the specific development of a family habitus of activism. For example, Rajinder (age thirteen) was born in Canada but his parents had moved here from India and Malaysia; both of his parents were highly involved within activist communities, opening opportunities for Rajinder to also become so engaged. By the time I met him at the age of thirteen, Rajinder was chairing meetings, had his own radio show, and was an active and vocal member of a number of activist organizations. Rajinder was an incredibly articulate young man, and had a strong grasp of many of the theoretical arguments that structured activist organizing; he could fluently cite Noam Chomsky, Gandhi, and Malcolm X, for example. Noteworthy was that he did not attribute his involvement in activist worlds to his parents' involvement at all, feeling that he had been the one to express initial interest, and they had simply supported him in this. However, in observing him and his mother cochair a meeting, it quickly became apparent to me that Rajinder did not stumble upon activist cultures in isolation from a wider family concern for social justice and activist engagement. Thus, although Rajinder's family migrated to Canada and likely shared many of the "race"- and class-based concerns that such a transition incurs, their own involvement and passion for social justice issues created a family habitus that permitted him to take up and expand those analyses within his own activist practices at a remarkably young age.

Class Injuries and "Performing Grunge"

The manner in which class is implicated within youth activist subcultures can similarly be traced through both the classed associations of historical and contemporary citizenship, and the specific manner in which class manifested within the subcultures themselves. In the first instance, class exclusions are strongly apparent in young people's experiences of schooling for citizenship, although often these exclusions were harder to identify. As a consequence, these experiences generally were not labeled as class-related by participants themselves. The hidden role played by class, which manifested as a form of class denial, further amplifies the kinds of injuries encountered, by remaining invisible and thus harder to both recognize and analyze. In particular, class plays a specific role in who can be an "active citizen" as exemplified within citizenship curricula and the wider cultural sphere. As Karen (age twenty-seven) so eloquently explains in the following excerpt, citizenship, as a function of active participation within a democratic public sphere, is simply not available to the majority of people in Canadian society or schooling, embedded as each is within consumerist codes of acquisition and the struggle for affluence in times of state retrenchment:

> *Karen:* I was never instilled with [democracy and citizenship] as a value... *Like, it was just always kind of latent, which is kind of problematic because everything else is so in your face.* Like, if that's latent and you're being told all the time to buy this to

be better or to, you know. Really I think the pressure of our generation was, you know, our parents were really worried that we're not going to have as much money as them. *And so they're like, just concentrate on yourself.* Do good work after that. *But just get yourself on your feet.* And when that's the predominant message, where is any of this caring stuff going to come from? *Kids who did caring stuff, kids who were involved in high school were kids trying to pad their resume.* (Emphasis mine)

The hidden text within this excerpt is the importance of class concerns in the production of the "good citizen." Karen comes from a white working-class/working-poor background; when she describes her parents as being concerned that she make more money than them, she is describing a reality that belongs, in this case, to a working-class family struggling to survive in the face of neoliberal retrenchment.[7] When she speaks of "kids trying to pad their resume," she is obliquely referencing the class divisions that continue to persist in education's production of the "active citizen" (through, for example, community projects), whereby those with middle-class aspirations and habitus learn early how to play the game of the "good citizen" in order to make themselves and their CVs more marketable in the "new global economy."

The opportunity to participate as an "active (and thus good) citizen" through community engagement projects cannot be uncoupled from young people's experiences of class and economic stratification in schools. Caleb (age twenty) spent most of his secondary education in a wealthy urban public high school. He then switched in his last year to another urban high school that was designated a "technical" school, which catered to a student population with a lower socioeconomic status. He marveled at the differences between the two schools in terms of both their academic expectations and their emphasis on community involvement:

Caleb: I went from Uptown Academic to Downtown Tech and I became a visible minority at the school. So that was, that was a difference.
Jackie: Who were the majority?

Caleb: Ah. Everyone else. No one, no one was really the majority but I mean.
Jackie: People of colour?
Caleb: Yeah. You know, everyone who I mostly didn't see at Uptown Academic. And you know the differences in everything in that school were huge. One of the things that I got from just going there for four or five months was that supposedly the public education system is an equal playing field between all schools, which is, I mean, between the two schools that I attended, is total bullshit. Like the kids at Downtown Tech are not stupid. They're smart guys. But the course load and the material and everything that they take that is the same is geared towards less critical thinking, less work, less difficulty, which just sets them up for not being able to work at the same level as people from Uptown Academic. Which outraged me, it really pissed me off. And at a community level it's the same thing. There's very little of it. There's no kind of organizing principle... So I mean if students were interested in activism it would be that much harder for them to get organized.

Caleb's experiences within the two schools highlights the division that exists between lower-resourced "technical" schools that historically serve working-class communities versus middle-class "academic" schools that can afford to focus on community involvement as an aspect of "good citizenship." Even farther along the same spectrum are the elite private schools, and the role they play in preparing young people to be "active citizens" through participation in community events. Jonathon (age twenty-five) attended such a school, an exclusive all-boys private school where, in his words, "they basically train you to be masters of the universe." He described the opportunities that were available to him because of his attendance there:

Jonathon: But I think that's essentially one of the problems, right? Is you know we had access to this really great education, but that's because, I mean, it cost fifteen to twenty thousand dollars a year. So we had opportunities. I mentioned that I was able to work on the yearbook and manage the theatre and all of this. And, yeah, I mean I had so many opportunities in high school. When I was in grade nine I was on the rowing team and I was responsible for a $30,000 racing hull and a crew of eight people. Right? I think that's had a huge impact on why I do what I do or where I am where I am. I had those opportunities.

Again, we see the elision of elite or higher-resourced schooling with opportunities for, if not activism, then certainly community engagement, as well as the development of skills and knowledge that could be of use within activist frames. Jonathon himself acknowledges that his elite education gave him the skills and aptitudes that permitted him to do the kind of activist work with which he was engaged.

What young people's experiences highlight is that attainment of the skills of "good citizenship"—which were sometimes identified by participants as one of their own stepping stones into activism—is often inextricably linked to one's location in a class-stratified society. Although it is important not to elide these kinds of community projects with activist engagement (see also Lousely 1999), the promotion and development of skills that are transferable to activism were often experienced by participants as linked to schools in middle- and upper-class neighborhoods. This accounts, in some part, for how class location has come to be implicated in *who* is able to develop the complex skills necessary to "belong" within activist circles.

It also points to the hidden elements of class that remain within the contemporary construction of the "good citizen." Again, showing remarkable continuity with the exclusions of the past, the increasing emphasis on particular kinds of community involvement (generally not activist) means that citizenship comes to have classed connotations. Similar to "race"-based exclusions, this functions as a form of governance by generating a set of feelings—that one is not good enough or not skilled enough to do community work and thus fulfill one's citizenship obligations, for example—that can cause some young people to "opt out" of engaging in this manner. Returning to Bourdieu's (1997) concept of symbolic capital, and the related term of symbolic violence (Bourdieu 2006 (1977); Bourdieu & Wacquant 1992), we can begin to see how this happens. Symbolic violence refers to how seemingly benign symbols—for example, that of the "good citizen" engaged in community work—can come to represent the symbolic hierarchies that configure our society, not explicitly but implicitly marking who has attained the forms of cultural capital that make it possible to perform the task of citizenship at this complex level. Bourdieu (1997) suggests that there exists a relationship between subjective expectations and objective chances, which attests to the remarkable consistency with which people will aspire only to the degree that the social structures permit—that is, they seem to be "choosing" particular goals, but these goals are aligned with those generally attributed to their class.[8] By linking something as seemingly benign and beneficial as "community projects" to "good citizenship," contemporary education functions to reinforce the symbolic domination of the middle classes who are easily able to participate in such projects as well as reconstituting the objective positioning of young people who seem to "opt out" of such acts of "good citizenship."

The role of class is thus obscured through a variety of mechanisms, which helps to explain why class was rarely remarked upon as an explicit category of analysis within the interviews and focus groups. Perhaps the most powerful means through which class roles were rendered invisible, however, was through the unspoken subcultural rules of youth activism itself. This is because the means by which young activists acquire the most subcultural capital within activist circles is by carrying out a *working-class performance*, one that often belies their own middle-class histories. As Andrew (age twenty-eight) notes:

> *Andrew*: I think some people, when they become radical politically, they try to deny that they're middle class or that they came from that kind of background. And they go to sort of weird lengths. Like maybe they intentionally work at a lower-paying job or dress poor. I find that really ridiculous. Middle class people who have to dress poor. Maybe that's the fashion in certain circles, but to me it's like kind of dishonest or whatever. I am relatively broke now because I spend a lot of time on activism or because I'm at school now. But I think to try to put myself on par with someone who actually grew up poor or like, I still have the security of coming from a middle class family and you have all of that I guess it's like self-confidence. You have that to fall back on.

Farah, who was one of the few participants to grow up in a politically active working-class immigrant family, reflects on the contradictions she experienced within activist circles, especially once she took a paid position in an activist organization:

> *Farah*: But when you're on salary and you're doing organizing—it just changes everything. You know?
> *Jackie*: How does it change it?
> *Farah*: I don't know like I, philosophically I have not been able to wrap my head around it. I'm still in the early stages of trying to figure it out. I've had good conversations with people about it. And feel better about it for a little while, but it never lasts. Um, I guess activism for me was about sacrificing. It was about being ah, like being on welfare as much of like a contradiction and this may sound like it. It was a way of dropping out of the society to be able to do something that no one else would pay you for, or no one else would value right? And there was sort of like this self righteousness in it and there was sort of this downward mobile bullshit about it too. But whatever it was, it was kind of where I come from especially organizing mostly in like white culture or punk rock activism—you know where most are middle class and white and go on welfare to organize or whatever.

Farah's experience of activism, with its expectations of personal sacrifice and its emphasis on downward mobility, were echoed by Karen, herself from a white working-class history:

> *Karen*: I mean I think that it's like, you know, (*laughs*) I feel this pressure to live without comforts. I mean, I think that activism taught me to appreciate really simple things, which is great. Which is really important to, like, unhook yourself from the cycle of material culture and accumulation that is North America. But it's like, you know, toast and tea for breakfast, supper and dinner does not a sustaining diet make (*laughs*). It was just like, you know, everything that you wear has to be free or second hand, you could never own a house because ownership, property is theft. Everything in your life needs to be really difficult (*laughs*). And, joy can only come from really simple, free things.

Karen goes on to describe her own struggle with these expectations and what they meant for her lifestyle and personal choices, particularly when they clashed with the doxa of the youth activist subcultures of which she was a part:

> *Karen*: These expectations that the domestic is really base, I found kind of, sometimes difficult. Because at the end of the day I was like, I just want a home. Like, not to buy a home, but I just want a home. I just don't want a punk rock crash pad any more. You know what I mean? I don't know. Who's that person on the couch? Don't know. (*Laughter*) I'd like to know. Would like my house not to be falling apart all around me and have a slumlord and you know, if that means paying more than $200 a month for rent that's going to have to happen. And I think that there was always also a set kind of prescribed group of things that you could do as recreation. It was like, hiking okay. You know, riding your free bike, okay. Going to protests, okay. And, going to see [punk rock band] Submission Hole, okay. Like, these are the four things that you can do. (*Laughing*)

The pressures and expectations as described here by participants were often bewildering, and, as Farah suggests ("philosophically I have not been able to wrap my head around it"), participants were often at a loss to explain why these rules existed, other than through a general recourse to anticonsumerism. While anticonsumerism as a political position may be one aspect of these subcultural forces, I suggest that Bettie's concept of class performance is a theoretical tool that can perhaps offer new insights into this phenomenon.

As described earlier, Bettie understands the "class performance" as one way to explain how people from one class of origin might "perform" a different class culture. Whereas in her work she focuses mostly on "middle-class performers"—those working-class young people who could disguise their class history by mobilizing middle-class symbols such as success in school—in the case of my study it tended to be middle-class young people taking on a working-class identity, or "performing grunge," as I have called it. The accounts presented here offer a glimpse into what shape these subcultural pressures take for young people involved in activist worlds. The belief that one must live without material comforts, and that in order to be a good activist one must make "sacrifices," is part of a constellation of expectations that mark whether one "belongs" within activist cultures. It also sits in interesting contrast to the larger cultural pressures to consume, whereby the activist subcultural stance against consumption becomes its own form of revolt. While the cycles of consumption within Canada may well be a pressing political issue, the problem with "performing grunge" is that it succeeds in returning the meaning of activism relentlessly and repeatedly to one's personal identity. The way in which one situates oneself within the internal power relations of activist cultures marks how well one has absorbed the unspoken cultural norms that allow one to "belong" or not. What this does is conflate the notion of social change and social movements with a misconceived emphasis on one's personal attributes—a regime of emphasis that is easily reconciled within a neoliberal ideological space that asks the subject to be forever self-perfecting. That the forms of self-perfection that young activists take up have more to do with downward mobility than competing in a global economy does little to reduce the class and "race" harms that such performances accrue.[9]

The array of symbolic markers that I have identified as "performing grunge," or enacting a working-class performance, can be particularly bewildering for people who come from working-class or working-poor backgrounds trying to penetrate activist life worlds. Luisa (age twenty) related a story of being questioned by a fellow activist for working part-time at McDonald's (which is not considered an appropriate job within activist circles, despite its low wage). This person expressed disbelief that Luisa could be working within the anticorporate activist milieu and still be employed at such a symbol of multinational corporatism. Luisa, however, saw it as a necessary job to help out her family, who had recently migrated from Latin America, and were faced with the challenges of establishing a stable income to support her and her siblings (note here again the elision between class, ethnicity, and histories of migration). Karen, who describes her family as "every day they're just gripping, just above the poverty line, like their necks sticking out," offers the following story:

> *Karen*: It's really funny, like [my friend], for example, we agree on a lot of different things, and have some sort of similar politics and friends and like that, but I remember she was like "we always had books in the house. And whenever we were out and we wanted a book, our parents would never deny it to us," and kind of thing? And I think we had this thing, and she was like, "it wouldn't matter, I would never be denied books." I was like "well, we couldn't afford books." She was like, "no, we just wouldn't be denied." And it was like, yep, no. And it was kind of this weird thing too, she was kind of making this value judgment? And I was like "food, books" [hands indicate weighing each], and we went with food. So I don't feel like I can be totally open with those things. You're just like, well, it's not gonna come up, and I'm not gonna bring it up, because I just don't think people would understand.

As Karen notes, a common strategy for navigating the class harms encountered in the middle-class world of activism was to "not... bring it up," where "it" becomes one's own history of poverty or struggle. Ironically, while middle-class people are busily disguising their middle classness, those from families with lower socioeconomic status may also be involved in similar processes, the result being that nobody is able to "be totally open about things." In talking to another activist about this phenomenon, himself from a working-class background, he suggested that middle-class people may sometimes feel self-conscious about their class backgrounds, and thus treat others with derision. He notes the subcultural capital that has come to be associated with this sort of working-class performance, linking it to activists being concerned with the question of "who is the most radical?" (Jean-Paul, field notes, Jan 3, 2007). Being "radical" is precisely the status that is most highly prized within youth activist subcultures, and its acquisition comes only to those capable of mobilizing the complex set of cultural resources that mark one as "in the know" (Thornton 1996) within youth activist subcultures. While Jean-Paul attributes the anxiety about being "radical" to "self-consciousness" and an accompanying sense of insecurity on an individual level, I am more interested in what this widespread phenomenon means on a more cultural-sociological level; that is, I want to ask what purposes does it serve, and what can it tell us about the complex relationship between class and young people's participation in activist cultures within the contemporary nation-state?

One response to these questions lies in considering the implications for activist subcultures of the particular contexts that have been described throughout the book so far. From neoliberal cultural formations to histories of class and "race" exclusions, to the contemporary pressures to perform a certain kind of "good citizenship," young activists are navigating a very complicated cultural field. What does this mean for who is granted the right to participate within youth activist subcultures, and who, on the other hand, may feel like an outsider to youth activist subcultures? To address this question from within a cultural sociological framework, I use Bourdieu's notion of *authorized language*.

Regimes of Symbolic Authorization: Consumption, Activism, Identity

Bourdieu describes authorized language as the means within stratified societies whereby particular actions become imbued with particular meanings because of the differing regimes of legitimation that are attached. In *Language and symbolic power* (1991), he notes that "a performative utterance is destined to fail each time that it is not pronounced by a person who has the 'power' to pronounce it, or, more generally, each time that the 'particular persons and circumstances in a given case' are not 'appropriate for the invocation of the particular procedure invoked'" (111). Authorized language is closely connected to cultural capital, and, in this case, subcultural capital, whereby it is those with the appropriate cultural capital within the appropriate context (or field) whose utterances are given greater legitimacy.

Authorized language is primarily cultural, in that its authority is derived from cultural and historical discourses that offer it legitimacy while simultaneously masking its embeddedness within regimes of inequality. One classic example of authorized language is the process of christening a new boat. I randomly choose a boat in the local marina, walk up to it, and smash a bottle of champagne on its side, declaring that it is now named the *Jackie Schooner*. Has the name of the boat changed? Not at all. But were the owner of the boat to take the same action, within the appropriate context and with the sanction of the appropriate boat-naming bodies, the boat's name *would* be changed. The utterance might be the same, but the outcome is different, depending on the legitimation structures attached to she who makes the utterance.

The ways in which authorized language manifests within activist subcultures is twofold. On the one hand, as described earlier, youth activism within Canada is often carried out by middle-class young people on behalf of those without such cultural capital. The discomfort that many young people feel with this dynamic was articulated by Tracey (age twenty-nine):

> *Tracey*: [F]or instance if I'm a person who's going in to collect my welfare cheque and they won't give it to me and I make a scene in the office—am I an activist? Or am I just getting my cheque? [W]hereas you know I turn up and I'm like: give her her cheque you know, I'm not leaving your office. Have I helped? Yeah I have but tomorrow I don't feel like showing up. You know it's kind of like really external and not that I, like—believe me I'm all for showing up at the welfare offices. I have no qualms of doing that but I'm just always conscious of the fact that I could leave. But you know, this is so difficult, it's so difficult coming from places, like I embarrassingly put myself [in the focus group drawing] kind of close to the state because, as much as I'm constantly like anti-state, anti-state, anti-nation, if I changed my mind tomorrow I could go and integrate fairly well, you know, I've got the education, I've got the background and I've got all of the things that would allow me to move into this kind of sphere. And I of course choose not to. I more than choose not to—I'm actively involved in trying to undo these things. But, you know you can never work that quite out, like when you have that possibility, I really struggle with [it].

Tracey here highlights an important element of the forms of authorized language carried by young people engaged in certain forms of activist work in Canada, whereby they can opt to make use of their privilege in the world to enact change. Indeed, this is often a conscious strategy used by activist groups—for example, Canadians accompanying people in other countries who might be the target of state violence (such as union organizers or human rights workers). The elements of symbolic authorization that young people embody and perform in activist circles are often inseparable from the kinds of work that Canadian activists do—and likewise often inseparable from the middle classness of the activists themselves, granting them the symbolic authority that they strategically draw upon. It is important to note that this is a context unique to only particular forms of activism—the activism that originates within communities that have been impacted takes a completely different shape (e.g., Aboriginal communities setting up road blockades in support of land claims disputes). However, the popular idea of "the activist" within the Canadian imaginary, I would suggest, is of one who is acting on behalf of others, a legacy that has much to do with liberal individualism, the constitution of the "good citizen" through community engagement, and the class heritage that supports these forms of activist practice. That this remains the dominant manner in which activism is understood and enacted was constantly being negotiated by the participants within this research.

This wider context of authorized language is not the only one within activist subcultures. Used less consciously and strategically, and inseparable from the middle-class culture that dominates youth activism, there is also an authorized language of the subculture itself, which incorporates the rules of comportment and demeanor that are policed, in a variety of ways, by the subcultural members. Ironically, given the emphasis on resisting North American consumption practices described earlier, the ways in which the symbolic authority of particular actors is reinforced is through specific consumption practices, as well as accompanying sets of beliefs and experiences. Conrad identifies some of the salient rules of comportment and consumption in the following excerpt:

> *Conrad*: One was like this identity thing where, on the one hand, I'm not like everybody else around me in these groups, and two, it's like, they're living this radicalism that I sort of, I'm not there, on that level, right? I'm not a vegetarian, like, I drive my car, right? How do I resolve that conflict in myself, I still have it right? But it's just like I can't do anything in Richmond, I've always hated that part of Richmond, like I always wish I could be in Vancouver, but then there's family responsibilities to help out there, and I can't, it's just a luxury often times, I think, that you have right? That's why I'm always like, if I didn't have a car, I wouldn't be able to go to these meetings, or these rallies or whatever.

Conrad here identifies that elusive quality, so desirable within youth activist subcultures, of "radicalism," and then traces some of the salient qualities that marks one as having achieved this status, including vegetarianism and not driving a car. His struggle is obvious here, where he notes, for example, that being without a car would significantly curb his activist involvement, given that he lives far from the urban center where most such events take place.

Rose (1999) sees consumption practices as becoming increasingly inseparable from the idea of the "active citizen" beginning in the 1980s. These "active citizens" were not expected to be active in the sense of participating within a political public sphere, but, rather, were to become "active" in their own self-regulation, "seeking to enhance and capitalize on existence itself through calculated acts and investments" (164). Rose (1992) notes that these new "active citizens" were located within a cultural field marked by the:

> proliferation of new apparatuses, devices and mechanisms for the government of conduct and forms of life: new forms of consumption, a public habitat of images, the regulation of habits, dispositions, styles of existence in the name of identity and lifestyle. In this new field, the citizen is to become a consumer, and his or her activity is to be understood in terms of the activation of the rights of the consumer in the marketplace. (164–165)

Following Rose, I would suggest that the struggle so eloquently captured by Conrad in the preceding excerpt can be best understood as one manner in which liberalism and, more relevantly, neoliberalism have penetrated youth activist subcultures: consumption practices, and what they mean for rituals of style and struggles for belonging, cannot be separated from the forms of "active citizenship" identified by Rose as becoming increasingly about one's identity as a consumer.

The links between activist identity, lifestyle, and consumption practices were strongly marked throughout my year of fieldwork. Not only did we discuss these issues during the interviews, but the impact of youth activist cultures noticeably permeated my own behavior within the field, shaping everything from the clothes I wore to the topics I would speak about outside of the more formal context of the interviews and focus groups. Such rules of comportment are common across all fields, as Bourdieu would suggest, although of course the specific rules change. My consciousness about my appearance was not particularly different than it is when I am in different settings (at an academic conference, say), but the specific items I chose to represent myself attempted to follow the subcultural rules of activist cultures, as I understood them. That such comportment might be important was noted by people other than myself; while staying at a friend's place in Montreal during my fieldwork, she commented that the outfit I was wearing that day was "perfect for doing interviews with activists"—I was wearing khaki cargo-style pants, a long-sleeved shirt underneath a short-sleeved red t-shirt that had an image of "Serpentina" on the front, a sort of carnivalesque cartoon of a woman with a snake wrapped around her neck (field notes, November 10, 2006).

The experiences of self-regulation and disciplining by others to ensure compliance with specific consumption practices and behaviors were described by many of the research participants. For example, Suzie spoke of feeling "vegan policed," and being terrified to host meetings at her home for fear of providing the wrong food. Diane described such activist "creds" as how many times you have been arrested, and for how long; "You have to look a certain way; you have to know certain people," she noted. The particular "look" that young people need to have in order to "fit" within activist subcultures was described by various people to include wearing used clothing, dressing in black, wearing political t-shirts, wearing sweatshop-free products, and just generally not looking "mainstream":

> *Jackie*: What was the dress code?
> *Phillipe*: You know. Like, nothing fashionable. You buy stuff like second-hand.
> *Jackie*: Second-hand, right.
> *Phillipe*: Yeah, like wool sweaters and non-conventional pants.
> *Jackie*: No brand names?
> *Phillipe*: No brand names at all. No logo. (*Laughing*)
> *Jackie*: Right. No logo of course.[10]
> *Phillipe*: I still kind of do that. It's not like my social group demands me to do it but still. If I was to come with a Nike cap to a meeting of [the organization I am involved with] I don't think people would like it a lot. (*Laughing*)

From another participant:

> *Angelina* (age twenty-one): T-shirts that have a message that is activist or political. You wouldn't dress in a way that's very mainstream. I think there's different ways of showing that or whatever. But it wouldn't be whatever the stereotypical like mainstream is. The way to dress—you wouldn't dress like that. Like, you know, try and [use] products that are sweat[shop] free or whatever.

Along with perceived rules of apparel, many participants commented that they felt there were a set of political beliefs and ideals that needed to be followed:

> *Daniel*: There's definitely a sense of expectations, that if you believe this, therefore you believe that, and I feel that in many ways I don't like this. You know, it's very much a herd mentality that causes people to go along with—[similar to] the Bush administration and causes people to support the war in Iraq, and the patriotism now that's going on in the United States is totally like a mass mentality, and there's a sense of not thinking for yourself, and just following, you know? But then on the Left, on the anti-establishment, there's the exact

same mindset. They're following different [ideas], [but] people who consider themselves non-conformist are very often just conforming to a different set of ideals.

Taken together, this package of beliefs, consumption practices, and apparel serves to constitute a particular type of recognizable "insider identity," one that provides the familiar legitimacy of group membership, and carries a set of inherited codes that come with an associated sense of belonging. Conrad described the youth activist identity as follows:

> *Conrad*: It's political, right? Always. And, that's the box though, is that it's about rallies, protests, and your complete refusal of things. That's why I have a hard time accepting it, because my youth activist [identity], is like [different from] those people that are in those [protests] that I go to, or I have a meeting with them all the time, so yeah, I guess I am [an activist], but I don't look like that, I'm not dressing like that, I'm not there, I have my car, all those things. So it is this total identity. And not just like what you're doing.

The implications of this code of beliefs, consumption practices, and style were that people who were unable to fulfill such requirements maintained structures of feeling that played against their feelings of inclusion and recognition within the youth activist subcultures:

> *Angelina*: I would say that it has impacted it in that I worried I wouldn't fit or something. Which is stupid 'cause it shouldn't really matter like what you know ... And that if I don't look exactly [like] they are or whatever, or if I don't believe in all those things, what does that mean? I don't know. Like when I was at the anti-imperialist march and there's people at [my university] I recognize who I'm friends with or whatever. But then it's like...just activists [are there]. I'm like, there should be more people here than just [activists]—how many people like imperialism (*laughing*)?...You know? Why aren't there more people out?...I don't know. It's just like you only march if you're part of the activist community and otherwise you just stay away even if you believe that.

What function do these unwritten "rules" and deeply coded behaviors play in disciplining the participation of specific people within activist cultures? As I have already suggested, I am not attempting to argue for the potential merit or disadvantages of such behaviors within the frame of activism. Rather I am more concerned with the emphasis on *individual choice* that such subcultural rules reinforce, and how this can be understood within the high modern, neoliberal context of the contemporary Canadian nation-state. As Hannah Arendt would suggest, when an individual's capacity to "act" within the public sphere becomes conflated with his or her personal identity and consumer choices, the space for ethical engagement within the polity is narrowed. In other words, the political realm, what Arendt saw as the true sphere for the enactment of "freedom," is turned into the space of what she calls the "social"—that is, the space where concerns about behavior and identity take primacy over any form of real ethical action (see Young-Bruehl 1982, 320). This has implications for the ways in which social change is both imagined and enacted through the activist subcultural communities themselves. As Nikolas Rose (1999) remarks,

> The problem of freedom now comes to be understood in terms of the capacity of an autonomous individual to establish an identity through shaping a meaningful everyday life. Freedom is seen as autonomy, the capacity to realize one's desires in one's secular life, to fulfill one's potential through one's own endeavours, to determine the course of one's own existence through acts of choice. (84)

When the emphasis for social change becomes inextricably linked to one's personal identity and individualized choices, the focus shifts from collaborative action based on solidarity and shared principles to judgments (of self and others) about one's capacity to fit within an imagined activist ideal. Luisa describes her experiences arising from this misplaced focus:

> *Luisa*: I had a lot of friends who would do little things like "Oh Luisa, I thought you were into saving the world." You know "what are you doing showering twice a day, aren't you supposed to be sustainable," like "why are you drinking coffee

at Starbucks?" And I think that comes from a very individualistic analysis of change, and that change is made on an individual level, [rather] than the collective level.

Taken together, what these remarks signify is the problematic emphasis upon individual choice as the apparent or most legitimate path to "freedom" (or justice, or social change). This particular discourse, with its deep roots within traditions of liberalism, is particularly dominant in Canada. Not only does it valorize individualized actions over those of collectives, but it also serves to mask other aspects of activist cultures, such as the impacts of class and "race" conflicts. While such specific consumer choices can, perhaps, be used as a strategy to leverage change directed at, for example, corporations (see Edwards and Mercer 2007), if these consumer choices begin to elide with one's sense of identity and self-worth, then the entire apparatus of social movements begins to shift toward a sectarianism that acts against the impulse for broad-based change (see also Zizek 2005). If the impetus for social change is to be found solely within one's personal identity and consumption choices, then arguably the foundations for a social movement will be fragile and impermanent, leading more equivocally to such emotions as guilt and anxiety over and above any capacity for recognizing and acting upon injustices.

Conclusions

The symbolic economy of youth activist subcultures exists within a specific, stratified cultural milieu, one that is highly permeated by histories of liberalism and contemporary neoliberal ideologies and is equally impacted by the class and "race" inequalities that exist in our wider society. Earlier in the book, it was established that this is a cultural space with a long history and a specific set of implications for young people attempting to locate themselves within the current political milieu of the contemporary Canadian state, as seen through the "detour" of the construction of the good citizen. The impacts of this cultural milieu are felt by youth activists through a variety of means. First, the histories of class and "race" stratification shape who has access to the specific habitus of activism today. Second, the effects of neoliberalism are felt through its emphasis on self-perfection and identity as expressed through consumption practices.

It is in these ways that the efforts of young activists to work for positive social change is undermined and complicated, in part through the very desire of individuals to *not* perpetuate the class and "race" distinctions that mark Canadian society. They do this by taking up practices that are intended to be ethical and anticonsumerist; however, when these practices are combined with a specific class and "race" background shared by the majority of people within this subculture, the assumptions of a "common sense" shared by all becomes (invisibly) laced with class and "race" concerns. For example, where one's actions or dress might suggest a lower socioeconomic status (because clothing is scruffy or patched, or one is living collectively in inexpensive housing, for example), one's academic or professional attainments, and the accompanying cultural capital that this accrues, mark a very specific subcultural identity that is only attainable by a limited few. If one wears only used clothing, but can cite Gramsci and Chomsky at will, where does one rest within a stratified society?

It is important to emphasize here that this manifestation is not the result of any one individual's will; that is, this circumstance has not come about because of a few thoughtless people who have intentionally perpetuated class harms. Rather, I am trying to point to the structure of feeling that exists within youth activist subcultures, one that runs deeper than any one individual's behavior or influence. That is, this is a *cultural phenomenon*, one that has an impact on anyone who enters into youth activist subcultures. I also played this game, even with the best of intentions not to, every time I entered into activist spaces. There are multiple times documented within interview transcripts when I found myself establishing my activist "creds" by pointing out the connections I had to people who were mentioned, or the knowledge I had about specific issues. While such a strategy could be helpful, on a methodological level, for establishing a sense of rapport and connection with my participants, more often than not it could also serve to reinforce differences in our relative acquisition of (sub)cultural capital. The desire to establish my credentials was strong, particularly if I was feeling insecure or anxious about whether I was myself being perceived as sufficiently "radical." Such is the way in which these structures of feeling play out at the level of the every day—by being expressed as embodied emotions that allow us to feel, as Bourdieu puts it, whether we are "in our place."

The point I am trying to make is that the regimes of symbolic authorization, including the practice of "performing grunge," cannot be pinned (or blamed, in other words) on specific thoughtless individuals. Indeed, to do so would be to misapprehend the very nature of this phenomenon. The point is that the subculture *acts through* the people who enter its space—that is, this phenomenon is not about individual character flaws, but about a specific cultural milieu that comes with its own rules and sets of behaviors—its doxa. My broader argument is that the specific shape that youth activist subcultures take within Canada are structured by a combination of a colonial past, a neoliberal present, and the ongoing stratifications on the basis of class and "race" that we currently live within.

The immediate question this raises, of course, is "how to change it?" If youth activist subcultural practices are excluding individuals because of this complex enactment of a "working-class/middle-class performance" that manifests as "performing grunge" and, as I am arguing here, this does not take place through any one individual's volition but through a structure of feeling, then where do we look to challenge this process? Where, in other words, does agency lie? As Bourdieu and others who have used his work (e.g., McNay 2000) have pointed out, understanding the durability of the habitus and the doxa that it produces highlights the sedimentation of social relations such that the potential for change can seem impossible. However, change *does* happen; within the context of this research project specifically, young people who were *not* from white, middle-class activist family histories or did *not* "perform grunge" still found their way into activist cultures. In order to explain this reality, and the potential to which it points, I turn in the next chapter to an exposition of *relational agency*, and its relevance for youth activist cultures, and social change more broadly.

5

BECOMING ACTORS: AGENCY AND YOUTH ACTIVIST SUBCULTURES

> To raise the question, what is freedom? seems to be a hopeless enterprise. It is as though age-old contradictions and antinomies were lying in wait to force the mind into dilemmas of logical impossibility so that, depending which horn of the dilemma you are holding on to, it becomes as impossible to conceive of freedom or its opposite as it is to realize the notion of a square circle.
> —Arendt 1968/1993, 143

The chapters preceding this one have focused on the reproductive and regulatory aspects of culture, the state, and education as they relate to young activists. They have subsequently neglected the creativity, possibility, uncertainty, and unpredictability that mark the cultural politics of youth subcultural activism. In this chapter, I attempt to remedy this exclusion, through an exploration of the cultural politics of action and agency within youth activist subcultures. While turning toward this aim, I seek to keep in place all of the important constraints that I have identified and theorized throughout the previous chapters; that is, in turning to agency, it would be disingenuous to suggest that all of the restrictive elements I have already identified do not continue to play an important and delimiting role in the cultural and social lives of young activists. Nonetheless, we are, and always will be, more than the structures that shape us, even if they intervene considerably in our lives. It is my concern here to consider the ways in which young people can come to articulate and express an activist identity, and ultimately to participate in specific forms of action within the public sphere, even in the face of wider social constraints, histories of liberalism and neoliberalism, moral claims and forms of surveillance about the apparently good citizen, and ideological apparatuses that caution young people to behave in certain ways or pay the price.

The theoretical articulation of agency that I develop in the pages to follow can perhaps best be understood as *relational agency*.[1] I situate this approach to understanding agency within the theoretical lineage of feminist political philosophy, beginning with the long-standing and sometimes bitter debates between Judith Butler and Seyla Benhabib about the origins of agency (see Benhabib et al. 1995). This debate has more recently been taken up by Lois McNay (1999a,b, 2000, 2003a,b, 2004) and Terry Lovell (2000, 2003), each of whom has attempted to move beyond the impasse that emerged between Butler and Benhabib by drawing upon other theoretical tools, including most prominently those of Pierre Bourdieu. Although I suggest that relationships, and the interactional structures that sustain them, are an essential component of political agency (or the capacity to take action within the public sphere), Bourdieu's conceptual frame can help to explain how this occurs from within a specific set of social interactions; that is, the interconnections between Bourdieu's concepts of *habitus*, *cultural capital*, and *field* are an essential aspect of any attempt to theorize agency.[2]

In the pages that follow, I will outline the theoretical components that make up my intervention within this dialogue, beginning with a discussion of feminist philosophers' approaches, then describing my own contribution to this field. I then turn to the data in order to illustrate the microsociological configurations of these theoretical constructs.

Feminist Debates and the Relational Basis of Agency

A long-standing and lengthy debate about the theoretical basis for agency has emerged among feminist political philosophers since the mid-1990s; such a debate may have found its natural location among feminists because of their (our) explicit concern with social emancipation (Cornell 1995; London Feminist Salon Collective 2004). Some of the key exchanges in the debate can be found in the works of Benhabib (1999), Benhabib et al. (1995), Lovell (2003), and McNay (2000, 2003a,b, 2004). The crux of the early debates, most powerfully articulated by Judith Butler (1995a,b) and Seyla Benhabib (1995, 1999), circulated around the role of discourses in constituting particular selves or subjectivities.

Butler (1995a) argues that the idea of the subject, with its roots in the Enlightenment lineage of modernity, must be continually deconstructed in order to uncover the potentially oppressive elements of the subject's discursive constitution: "Paradoxically, it may be that only through releasing the category of women from a fixed referent that something like 'agency' becomes possible" (50). Benhabib (1995), on the other hand, remains unconvinced that Butler's formulation in fact yields such a possibility. At heart, her concern resides with a critique of Butler's performative model, querying "how can one be constituted by discourse without being determined by it?" (110). Instead, Benhabib (1999) offers a narrative model of identity that, she suggests, overcomes the dichotomy between the rational, Enlightenment self critiqued by feminists and the discursively constituted self proposed by Butler. In suggesting such a narrative model, she attempts to reintroduce a "stronger concept of human intentionality" (339).

Subsequent feminist theorists, including most notably Lois McNay and Terry Lovell, have more recently picked up where this debate left off. McNay (1999a,b, 2003a,b) suggests that neither Benhabib's nor Butler's approach provides a satisfactory account of agency, although she is appreciative of how each has moved the debates forward. She suggests that a more complex account of agency must incorporate both a dialectical account of temporality (following Ricoeur) and a generative account of the subject who not only acts in *reaction* to situations, but also responds creatively and innovatively (McNay 2000). She grounds her theory in Bourdieu's concepts of habitus and field, noting "the necessity of situating any theory of agency within the context of power relations if voluntarism is to be avoided" (162). In a subsequent essay, McNay (2004) begins to articulate a more explicitly relational account, noting that "it is Bourdieu's definition of his social phenomenology as relational that has interesting implications for a feminist analysis of gender as a lived social relation" (184).

Many theorists, feminist and otherwise, have remarked on the contribution of Bourdieu's sociocultural theory toward understanding human action (see, e.g., Dillabough 2004; McLeod 2005; Reay 2004; Sewell 1992). As Nick Crossley (2001) notes:

> What [Bourdieu's social theory offers is] a conception of human action that can account for its regularity, coherence, and order without ignoring its negotiated and strategic nature. This is what the concept of the habitus is designed to achieve. An agent's habitus is an active residue or sentiment of his [or her] past that functions within his [or her] present, shaping his [or her] perception, thought, and action, and thereby molding social practice in a regular way. (83; square brackets mine)

However, there is a dilemma that emerges whenever Bourdieu's concept of habitus is used to understand agency; that is, at what point does the creative self begin, and how does such creativity even become a possibility? Crossley states:

> Habits are sedimented effects of action, indeed of repeated actions, and any account of them therefore presupposes an account of action, such that action cannot be reduced to habit in the manner that Bourdieu sometimes suggests. In a sense, he recognizes this when he deems the habitus a "structured structure"; habits emerge, he argues, out of an agent's active involvement in a structured field of practice. This begs the question, however, of the agent who engages in a field of practice before they have incorporated its structures, so that they can actually incorporate those structures. How can we explain this pre-habitual action? (95)

Terry Lovell (2003) offers a theoretical account of agency, based on Bourdieu's work, that attempts to resolve this dilemma through a focus on agency as residing within a collective. Lovell suggests that in order to better understand the locus of agency, theorists must shift away from a "focus on 'the (subjected) self' [and focus instead] on the social relations of political (inter)action, and the specific historical conditions of particular social transformations" (2). She invokes the story of Rosa Parks, whose refusal to give up her bus seat to a white passenger was a pivotal moment in the struggle for African American civil rights in the mid-1950s. Drawing on Bourdieu's concept of authorized language, she argues that the success of this act must be understood within the context of the times, and that the specific moment in which it happened was as important as the fact that it happened at all:

> The authority of Parks's act of defiance was not endowed on it, as we have seen, by Parks alone, but by the endorsement and publicity given to it by the nascent civil rights movement and by the people who supported the boycott with such impressive solidarity and in the face of great personal hardship. (9)

On this basis, Lovell suggests that we must understand "effective political agency [as] interactional and collective" (14). She sees the success of Parks's act of resistance as inseparable from the collective response that it was given, noting that previous similar acts by other women and men did not receive the same response, and thus did not achieve the same effect.

This account provides an important shift away from the individual and toward the collective (and relational) aspects of agency. However, I would suggest that it does not, in fact, explain Parks's *agency*, that is, the decision she initially makes to refuse to give up her seat. Instead, it accounts for the strategic success of the move, rightly noting that the timing and larger community support made this risk on her part worth taking. However, an important aspect of the historical and biographical record describing Parks's act is missing from Lovell's account, a piece that might help explain Parks's capacity to remain in her bus seat in the face of tremendous potential sanctions. Parks, along with other leaders of the civil rights movement such as Martin Luther King, had attended the Highlander Folk School, a training ground for civil rights activists. She had also been a longtime member and secretary of the NAACP (the

National Association for the Advancement of Colored People; Highlander Research and Education Center 2005). As noted on the website of the Highlander School:

> Our society teaches history through stories of remarkable individuals, and while Rosa Parks was indeed remarkable, her story is also about collective action, willed risk, intentional plans and mass movement...At the time of her arrest, Rosa Parks was a respected community leader already working to counter humiliating racist laws and traditions. (Ibid.)

We might thus understand Parks's ability to take that action as coming out of her own history of participation in an organized movement of activists, a set of relationships that gave her the resources, knowledge, and capacity to take that enormous risk. Such an explanation looks toward the genesis of Parks's original act as belonging within a community of activists, rather than ascribing it either to an individual acting in isolation, or to a focus on the outcome of the act itself.

Indeed, it is the lack of a theoretical account of what McNay identifies as the generative and creative aspects of agency that, I would suggest, has characterized previous feminist accounts of agency. That is, as of yet no theory of agency can explain the modalities by which some people come to take specific actions (especially those actions that go against the grain of mainstream convention, or of their acquired habitus) while others do not. It is this gap that my account of relational agency, developed in light of ethnographic data on the lives of youth activists, is designed to address.

The first part of my theoretical framework for understanding agency begins with the assumption that for some people it is *easier* to become an activist than for others. This sense of ease comes from specific family histories of activism or left-leaning political affiliations, as well as a specific class and "race" background; in other words, an activist habitus. It is important thus to recognize the persistent role played by habitus in shaping young people's capacity to come to political action; while the story does not end there, it is certainly an important piece of the puzzle. However, there are those who come into activism via different routes—who appear to have rejected an earlier formed habitus (developed through a conservative family upbringing, for example), and thus undertaken a *habitus shift* that permits their involvement within the doxic field of Canadian youth activism. It is these people I am particularly interested in here, and the stories that they shared about what brought them into activism, and what allowed them to remain.

Although the habitus is intrinsically based on relationships (Lawler 2004; McNay 2004), it does not necessarily account for *how* those relationships might be established such that the agent is able to take actions that he or she might not otherwise have done. This is where an ethnographic and phenomenological account can contribute to a theory of agency, by revealing the modes by which young people make sense of their own capacity to act, or to become activists. While relational processes are certainly not the *only* manner in which young people come to participate in a public sphere of activist dissent on issues of war, globalization, poverty, or colonialism, their recurrence within my data indicates that relationships may be an overlooked resource in feminist debates about agency thus far. Relational agency, as I am using it here, can be understood as the contingent and situated intersection between an individual's social position within a field of interactions, and the means by which the relationships within that field permit that individual to take actions that might otherwise be inconceivable—or, in other words, permit them to achieve a habitus shift.

There are two main ways in which relational agency came to bear within my data: first, by mediating the acquisition of an activist habitus through participant experiences of being "invited in" to activist subcultures. Second, by constituting the community of relationships within which a newly emergent activist habitus could take root and find the support to both develop into further activist engagement and enable one to continue within an activist field that is often extremely challenging.

On Being "Invited In": Acquiring An Activist Habitus

Participants from nonactivist families reported that they often first entered the activist field by developing relationships with other young people who could act as a sort of "cultural guide" to the nuances of activist life worlds. Such an invitation was not a free-floating option available to all. The very process of "developing relationships" generally presupposes an experience of mutual commonality that is often mediated by social markers such as class, gender, and "race." That is, it becomes increasingly difficult to develop such relationships the farther one's habitus—or set of commonsense experiences and understandings about the world—is from that of the other person. Thus, while young people might not carry all of the markers of an activist habitus, they would generally share some set of experiences or outlooks that permitted the formation of those relationships in the first place. This opened up the possibility of being "invited in" to the activist field by friends, thus changing the very configuration of the habitus itself:

> *Will*: I think it really started when I went to Montreal. When I moved. It started out with some student groups, second, third, fourth year. I was more open to joining groups. Kind of like, I was feeling my way around. I mean, it was a new environment so it was kind of hard at first, but I started to attend more film screenings and more events and more meetings and…more organizing. And at the time I had friends who were in Montreal who were kind of immersed in that culture as well. I had a close friend who went to Concordia and was very active at Concordia so I kind of, you know, got pulled along the way, too. (*Laughs*)

Will's account highlights his already existing predisposition toward the activist field—what he describes as being more "open"—that developed during his time at university. Once this "opening" happened, it became easier to deepen relationships with the friends who "pulled [him] along the way."

Nancy (age twenty) similarly articulates her already existing predisposition that permitted the development of the relationships that led to an ever-deepening involvement in the activist field:

> *Nancy*: What happened? It had already been there. What was the motivation? Well I think it was just somebody inviting me to, something as simple as I was invited to a meeting.

Jackie: Like a friend invited you to a meeting?
Nancy: Yeah. It was probably a friend of mine and so it just sort of evolved from there and, yeah, that's just kind of how it happened. But, and the thing is though I had always been, even before then, in grade eight, I had already started to take some sense of ownership in school life and we had to organize a teachers' awards where we gave all of our teachers awards because, it was just like an idea. Oh, this will be something great, a great project to get involved in, why don't I start doing this? And then, I had always just kind of wanted to be involved with community life, you know? So.

In this case, Nancy's experience of being "invited in" to the activist field was preceded by the kinds of community projects consistent with the "good citizen" within educational and broader cultural discourses. As discussed previously, the opportunity to engage in such "good citizenship" projects can sometimes inadvertently lead to deeper engagement in activist life worlds, through the acquisition of applicable skills and knowledge. Thus a range of factors can lead to the development of a particular predisposition—or openness—that makes it possible to be "invited in" to activist subcultures and to feel capable of accepting that invitation.

This preexisting interest, combined with the experience of finding a "cultural guide," also provides the context for Jennifer's (age twenty-three) experience of becoming deeply involved in the anarchist and activist communities in Montreal. Her background did not particularly lend itself to this route; while carrying the class and "race" markers that still retain dominance within activist circles (i.e., she was white and middle class), she came from a politically conservative family in Alberta, attended a Catholic high school, and recalled no particularly politicizing experiences from her childhood and adolescence. None of her friends were political, nor was she connected to any activists within Calgary. The summer before she began at McGill, she received a notice from the university about her different options for "Frosh week," the orientation week for first-year students. She was allowed to choose whether she wanted to participate in the regular, mainstream Frosh activities, or instead take part in something called "Radical Frosh," which advertised itself as an alternative to Frosh week that was antiracist, antisexist, antiableist and so on, and not focused on alcohol and partying. She describes her decision to choose "Radical Frosh" as a difficult one, explaining her uncertainty about whether she would find people there who she could connect with:

> I knew I was interested in it, but I was like who's going to go to this, because at the time I didn't identify as anything queer or anything, so you have all these stereotypes, would they all be gay and lesbian, not drinking, all straight-edge type people. But all these things were very interesting to me, they had all these workshops, they seemed fun. And I had the Arts [orientation] to meet all the "normal" people.

She laughed at herself as she relayed this, admitting that now she too was one of the "radical queer" people, as were many of her friends. Her account also highlights the fear she felt when she thought she might not find people with whom she could relate within the "Radical Frosh" group—in other words, that she would not find people with whom she shared a meaningful habitus. Ultimately, however, "Radical Frosh" became her entry point into activism, because of the connections she made there and where they led her:

> And so through this is probably how it started, because I met a lot of my friends, who are still friends with me now, so five years later. Uh, one of my friends I met there...is...a great activist...really committed—he was involved [in Radical Frosh], and he grew up in Toronto, got involved with OCAP [Ontario Coalition Against Poverty]...and so he was very politicized. So we were hanging out and at the start of this school year...there was like this open meeting and mobilizing and talking about the FTAA [Free Trade Area of the Americas], and so John told me like, "you should come to this," so I was like "okay! I'll go!"...I was kind of scared, but it was the best way...I think I just learned so much, and met some really amazing people...in all different years of their education, and then yeah, from then on it was sort of like, I was in.

As her remarks suggest, becoming part of youth activist subcultures is often a clear experience of being "in" or not. Later in the interview, she describes how it was easier to attend activist events because there were people there who she had met during her "Radical Frosh" experience, and because she would always have friends attending events and meetings, so creating an incentive for her to go. Thus, she found her way into activist organizing through forming relationships with other people that gave her the opportunity to reconfigure the habitus she had acquired from a conservative upbringing into one more suitable to activist life worlds. However, as I observed through my field work and in the focus group, Jennifer appeared less certain of herself and her beliefs when in a room full of activists, speaking hesitantly and apologetically, if at all. One might assume that either the authorized language or the forms of symbolic domination in operation within the field of youth activism played some part here. The following is an excerpt from the Montreal focus group; I had just asked the participants to share the images they had created of their ideas about Canada as a state entity, and I asked Jennifer to describe hers to the group:

> *Jennifer*: So this one's really bad. I don't know. It's all the beautiful mountain-scape. We like our environment so much you know. But anyway it's kind of hard to think of what to do so I just—And I thought of diamonds and like Blood Diamonds. It's such a horrible film. I don't know if you figured—it really bothered me. It bothered me a lot. But no, just like the things people are watching on television—how horrible things are elsewhere and hoping we can change cause it's like (unclear) a lot of deceit. 'Cause then right behind them is everybody's house is being knocked down to build condos. (*Laughing*)... This is my nice Arabic looking guy with a gun. Who wanted um I don't know his money from wars going into everything from big business to universities. I don't know. That's what I—threw together.

As captured here, Jennifer opens and closes her description by apologizing for her work, beginning with "this one's really bad" and ending with "That's what I threw together." Another participant also noted this apologetic tendency, and commented that she had seen Jennifer do that elsewhere; this particular participant, who appeared entirely at ease within activist subcultures herself, commented that Jennifer "had a good analysis," but was unnecessarily shy about it. Drawing on Bourdieu's language, we might understand this as an instance of misalignment between habitus and field (see Adkins 2004)—perhaps Jennifer is not yet entirely certain of her "place" within the informal hierarchies that make up youth activist subcultures: in other words, she is not entirely certain of her status as "in."

This experience of being "in" and the implications it carries for participating in activism was echoed by Matthew (age twenty-nine). Matthew was born into an upper middle class family with a politically conservative father, but after his parents separated when he was twelve he lived with his mother who had to struggle to make ends meet. He described himself as on the edges of activist cultures in Vancouver, and felt that he had only recently encountered this subculture and started to participate in it because of his girlfriend, Rebecca. He also noted that he wasn't able to do much prior to two years before because he had been heavily addicted to drugs and had not yet come out as transgendered. Having both come out as trans and left the drugs behind, he described himself as better able to take part in activist worlds. Still, similar to the participants cited earlier, he notes that he had to be "invited in":

> *Matthew*: So I feel like I was just invited into it. And still Rebecca has to say to me like "why didn't you speak up and say that when we left? Why didn't you do this? Why didn't you?" Because I still don't feel like I have a place in it. So I think that that's just, you know, if I could change something that would be something to change. We need to invite more people into it. We need to tell them that it's okay for them to speak, to make those environments safe.

The experiences of both Jennifer and Matthew illustrate how the capacity to participate in activist life worlds—to be "invited in" and to feel that one belongs—often comes about through encountering other people with whom one feels a connection and who can help one navigate the cultural life world of youth activist communities. However, even the predisposition to seek out these circles comes from a particular history, one that often includes a set of experiences that makes activist work both conceivable and desirable. Neither this disposition nor the set of relationships that permits its development is available to all young people in equal measure. Thus it is important to keep in mind the interlocking impacts of both the cultural *predisposition* to take action (developed through an activist history within one's family or within one's own encounters with the world), combined with a set of relationships that permit one to take up and develop this capacity. Political action, in the form of activism in particular, seems to be especially linked to a set of relationships that provides the support and encouragement that permits one to take action—especially if those actions are personally risky. This is not surprising given the wider cultural sanctions associated with taking activism past the acceptable boundaries of the "good citizen." Indeed, this is part of the context that necessitates the formation of strong relational ties—generally through friendships or romantic involvement—that permit young people to move farther into the forms of oppositional practices that are vilified in the pages of mainstream media outlets such as Canada's national daily newspapers.

Relationships as Resource for Action

Beyond functioning as a starting point for activist involvement—through the experience of being "invited in"—relationships often permitted the participants to deepen their activist involvement, taking them past the culturally sanctioned boundary of "good citizenship" and into the realm of the "trouble-making activist" (as portrayed within wider cultural scripts). Patrick (age twenty-one), who comes from a left-leaning, though not activist, family, describes his own sense of moving toward being able to take personal and political risks, once he was embedded within a community of activists:

> *Patrick*: And then second semester the [student] strike happened and then I got involved—got to know people and then... they were planning the occupation [of an administrator's office]. And... you see that was funny because [another research participant] was one of the people doing that. And for him—he's somebody who's done this before and I was just like whoa. But it was a point where I was committed to

> doing the occupation. So that was kind of a step, like I was willing to do that. It didn't actually happen but—I was going to so that was kind of a point where I could take a step [and] be willing to do more stuff...And then I tell you the main outcome of the strike was knowing people from [student activist group] and then like the social aspects of that because that's basically what everything—all my friends were from that group of people and it all sort of came out of that.

Such friendship circles seem to play an integral role in the lives of many of the young people who participated in this project, supporting and enabling them to continue in the often fraught work of activism. Such networks also made organizing that much easier, in that they provided a ready made pool of people to draw upon to assist with actions or attend meetings, people who already shared worldviews and values and could be relied upon. I had the opportunity to witness such organizing at work one night in Montreal, while staying at the house of Christine (age twenty-six), a self-described anarchist organizer who has been carrying out actions since the age of fifteen. Deeply embedded in the activist communities in both Montreal and Toronto, she is an incredibly articulate, energetic, and charismatic force for social change. All of her roommates are equally engaged in various activist projects, and their house is a hub of meetings and events, and host to multiple traveling activists. I stayed the night there while in Montreal for this research, and was witness (and participant) to an impromptu organizing session around the kitchen table. We had just come from an event that evening related to the ongoing racist immigration policies in Canada, expanded after September 11, 2001. Four of us sat around the kitchen table, eating a late-night stir fry of chickpeas and vegetables: myself, Christine, her roommate Omar, and his girlfriend Evelyn. We were discussing the ongoing hunger strike of the men being held in the Kingston Immigration Holding Centre—called "Guantanamo North" by activists—and what to do to bring their plight to the attention of the general public. They were hunger striking in protest of conditions they were experiencing within the Holding Centre, where they had each been held for several years under the authority of the Security Certificates that had been introduced by the Canadian government after the terrorist attacks of September 11. None of them had been charged with any specific crime, nor had they been shown the evidence that the Canadian Security and Intelligence Service claimed justified their ongoing detention. As our kitchen table discussion ensued, the prisoners were heading into day seventy of their hunger strike. Omar, his face heavy with exhaustion, said, "They're going to let them die," the "they" in this case being the federal Conservative government. Christine kept urging us to consider the possibilities for action, reminding us that "we have to do something." The conversation ranged across options, Christine driving it with urgent questions about how to do something more original and strategic and attention-grabbing than another picket outside the Immigration office. We tried to think of high-profile government officials whose offices could be occupied. We discussed other creative actions that could be taken; maybe blocking traffic, maybe something in the Metro transit system. By the end of the night we had developed a plan for the following Tuesday, and Christine had composed an e-mail and sent it out to her lists of contacts.

What is noteworthy about this experience is the deeply embedded web of relationships that its success relied upon. This was not a public meeting called to include any who might be interested to come out and take part; the urgency of the issue and the nature of the action required that it draw upon an already existing network of like-minded people with shared knowledge and political commitments, and the capacity and skills to carry out an action such as this. While not all actions emerge in this way, the existence of a shared "common sense"—or doxa—and the relationships upon which this common sense was built, enabled the quick and effective organizing that took place that night around that kitchen table.

Relationships as Means of Exclusion: The Limits of Relational Agency

Situating relational agency from within Bourdieu's social theory implies the recognition of the structuring role relationships can also play. That is, while relationships might be understood as enabling action—including the development of a revised habitus as well as supporting political actions that are not condoned by the mainstream—they can also serve to reinscribe exclusions already existing within both activist subcultures and the wider cultural sphere. Returning to the earlier example that saw a group of four around a kitchen table, a private encounter within the confines of a home, it is easy to understand how difficult it can be for people who are not "in the know" to penetrate the subcultural walls of youth activism within Canada. One important aspect of these subcultural communities is the way in which word can spread within them, such that one's network becomes an integral way to receive information about actions and events in the first place. This excerpt comes from my field notes, while in Toronto, reflecting on a protest against the repression of dissent that was happening in Oaxaca, Mexico, at the time:

> I was thinking about the fact that it was all the same people at this event as have been at most of the events and meetings I've been to lately, which always seems to be the case, no matter what city—there's always the problem of preaching to the converted, which is part of how the whole activist culture gets cultivated. I was thinking also about how I am newly reimmersed in this activist culture in Toronto, talking to people and going to events, and so I am in the loop. This meant that I received word of this Oaxaca protest from no less than four different sources, plus saw signs up around my neighbourhood, plus received info on parallel Vancouver protests. [My partner], on the other hand, hadn't heard anything about Oaxaca, either the events or the protests. Something that I had heard of so often that it seemed it must be common knowledge was completely off her radar (and the radar of the vast majority). (Field notes, November 3, 2006)

The circles of information can thus function to develop a particular kind of "common sense," such that the activist habitus (just like all habituses) plays a reinforcing role, ensuring that those who share this "common sense" continue to do so, and those who are outside of it are unable to bridge the gap of intelligibility unless they, too, become part of these relational networks.

Such tight-knit networks, while providing the emotional and relational resources to become active, can thus also serve as a barrier to the inclusion of people who do not share the activist habitus. This comes about not through bad intentions on the part of those who are "in" but through the basic emotional response of ease that comes with finding like-minded people who share the activist habitus, in such a way that it is much easier to relate to one another:

> *Nancy*: Well there's two things, right? It's two-fold. It's activism and it's also values. So if you're not necessarily active but we share politics and if our value systems are similar in terms of social justice and equity and anti-oppression then we'll have a lot more in common and we can definitely relate, even if you're not active at all. So if you are both then we're really on the same page and that's the majority of my circle. And then, but if you're neither, it's going to be kind of hard to have a chat.

As Nancy (age twenty) notes, it can become difficult to relate to people outside the common culture of activist life worlds, and such difficulty in relating can serve as an emotional barrier to people who do not feel as if they "fit." Angelina (age twenty-one), a woman of color who comes from an upper middle class left-leaning family, discusses her experience of the exclusivity of certain activist groups:

> *Angelina*: Sometimes... I'm like wow I'm not part of any of these groups. So I feel weird about going just because... there are certain characteristics about how activists kind of, like the stereotype or whatever. And—like I'm not going to change myself to fit those. But at the same time it doesn't mean I don't believe in those things [i.e., activist values].
> *Jackie*: What are the characteristics of the activist stereotype?
> *Angelina*: Um, I think of some people—well at [my university] it would be, I don't know, people who like... well they're usually all friends with each other.

Angelina is describing a common experience among participants who were not quite "in" the center of youth activist subcultures. It was a feeling of being outside, of perhaps sharing values and beliefs, but, for whatever reason, not finding for oneself a sense of belonging and "fit" within these communities. Such an experience of "fit" was often mediated by such social markers as class and "race," and the ways in which these shaped the acquisition of an activist "common sense" or habitus. It was further mediated by the specific rules of comportment attached to the youth activist field, such as enacting an activist subcultural performance through attire and consumption practices. While Angelina continued to do her own activist work through other circles and community groups, she was still dogged by a sense of who properly "belonged" to activist subcultures. Angelina carried enough of the activist habitus from a left-leaning family and a politically engaged higher education to permit her to find other avenues of action, developed through different kinds of relationships. However, not all young people are able to muster the personal, cultural, and emotional resources available to her, especially when they feel shut out of the communities of activist practice where they might otherwise develop them.

One implication of such friendship circles standing in as proxy for circles of organizing colleagues (who might not necessarily be friends) is the way in which they can skip important steps in the process of collaborative work, so that people who do not feel a personal affinity with others in the room might feel unwelcome or unheard:

> *Vincent* (age twenty-six): I find if it's too friendly then there's less attention paid to internal processes and dynamics. So I mean there is this kind of tendency in, you know, quote "left-leaning" groups to just be like, we're all leftist so you know we don't need to do all this bureaucratic stuff. But you do need to do that stuff like, I mean, it's a double responsibility also you know, to try and get things done externally but to keep things right internally as well.

The flip side, then, of the kinds of relational and emotional resources provided by networks of friends engaged in activist work is how these can function to reproduce the exclusivity of activist circles, so that it can become increasingly difficult for those who have not had the opportunity to develop an activist habitus to become involved in this work. Such barriers emerge in various ways: because networks of friends keep each other informed of actions and events; because people feel more "at ease" with each other, and so are more likely to seek each other out; and because the friendship circles can result in a disregard for formal processes that might allow people who are not networked to become part of the activist work. Thus, while the potential to come to action is often cultivated and strengthened through relationships with networks of people already doing the work, such networks can also function to exclude those who have not acquired the appropriate subcultural capital, or the activist habitus, that allows such relationships to develop in the first place.

Conclusions

This chapter has considered the ways in which young people come to take action within the public sphere, which I have described, not unlike other theorists, as the performance of a specific modality of political agency (see, e.g., McNay 2000, 2004). I have described and attempted to expand upon a theoretical conception of agency that is, at its core, relational. To do so, I have drawn upon the theoretical work of feminist philosophers Lois McNay and Terry Lovell, as well as the cultural sociological frame of Pierre Bourdieu. Both McNay and Lovell have articulated a concept of agency that is interactional, bodily, and relies on a notion of the subject that is broader than the rational, choosing individual of the liberal state. Using their theoretical work as the basis for my own, I have demonstrated the manner in which such agency takes place within youth activist communities. I have suggested that young people, particularly those who have not developed an activist habitus through family, class, "race," and political histories, often find their way into activist circles through the experience of being "invited in" by a friend or romantic partner, noting that many young people experience activist subcultures as clearly having an "in" and an "out." The fact of this clear sense of being "in" (or not) further highlights the ongoing role of authorized language and subcultural capital within the activist field, and the role they play in regulating who might have access to the forms of community that appear to be necessary for effective activist organizing. I note the important role that friendship circles play in supporting young activists in their political work, as well as in providing the informational and emotional resources that permit young people to remain active and involved. However, I also point out that friendships can play a limiting role in *who* is able to access youth activist subcultures, in that they can exclude those who do not form these friendships, and thus do not have access to the information and support that permits involvement. Since friendships often emerge unconsciously along class, gender, and "race" lines—because the people with whom we feel "at ease" often share these characteristics with us—they can also serve to perpetuate the class-, gender- and "race"-based exclusions identified by participants in the previous chapter. Friendships can also act as a disincentive to follow group processes that might open up activist subcultures such that "outsiders" can become involved.

Having noted the role played by cultural codes of friendship and style, a judgment may be perceived here, one that suggests that activist subcultures ought to become more "open." However, it is important to note that it may not always be desirable or necessary for activist subcultures to do so, as the trust and reliance developed through networks of friendship built on experiences together might be pivotal, particularly for the more politically and personally risky actions undertaken by some young people trying to oppose particular state policies or practices. Nonetheless, when taken in combination with the classed and raced elements of youth activism in Canada, it is important that such relational practices be scrutinized for their oppressive potential. That is, it is my hope that by uncovering these aspects of youth activist practices, it will be easier for those within these circles to identify and challenge their own subcultures to remain as open as possible to the participation of as wide an array of young people as they can attract. This is the hope and the promise of democratic participation, an integral part of which are the kinds of political actions taken by the people who were involved in this research project.

Finally, to draw a more explicit line between the historical and contextual work of the previous chapters and this one, it is important to note how histories of colonialism, racism, and classism, as well as the predominant contemporary cultural pressures to be a particular kind of "good citizen," play into the modalities of relational agency available to young people. That is, there is a reason only a certain limited number of young people who are not from white, middle-class, activist families even consider the possibility of joining in dissident practices, let alone find the relational resources to become actively engaged. The wider cultural context remains one in which dissident participation such as activism is ridiculed, dismissed, and generally frowned upon. Young people's experiences within schooling of acceptable forms of citizenship participation are limited to placated versions of "responsible" action taken within a self-regulating neoliberal frame (see also Kennelly & Llewellyn, in press). In addition, the wider cultural sphere of submerged (and not-so-submerged) racism and classism means that some young people learn early on that they are not in a position to take up "active citizenship" (activist or not) within the frame of the Canadian nation-state. This is the manner in which the wider cultural sphere of mainstream notions of the "active citizen" combine with the exclusivity that can mark activist subcultural practices to render only certain limited numbers of young people access to the kinds of relational resources that can lead to activist organizing.

6

Conclusions

"Citizen Youth" and Implications for Social Change

Young people attempting to negotiate their relationship to the nation-state in Canada do so from within a specific cultural field, one that is burdened with histories that continue to resonate in the present, and political ideologies that shape both the contemporary moment and the future. They must confront first and foremost the construction of the "good citizen" as a cultural phenomenon that carries traces of Canadian classism, racism, and colonialism, the legacies of liberalism and neoliberalism, and a moral code that finds expression in the wider cultural sphere through such sites of representation as the media. The implications of this context—that is, of the cultural spaces within which young people might understand their relationship to the state—is that "activism," as one mode of democratic engagement with the public sphere, is placated through depoliticized references to charitable acts without critical scrutiny, and offered as a liberal means by which the individual might assuage his or her sense of responsibility to the state. Such placation takes place even while certain forms of activist engagement—particularly those that challenge state structures and authority—are curtailed or misrepresented through structures such as policing and media. "Youth activism" has thus come to carry multiple codes of meaning, understood as both a desirable goal (within the construct of the apolitical "good citizen") and demonized as an irrational and irresponsible mode of "troublemaking."

Into this cultural fray enter the youth activists. For this research, I focused on groups that I saw as acting in general opposition to the state—antiglobalization, antipoverty, antiwar, and anticolonialism activists—in order to better understand how they made sense of their own relationship to citizenship, to the state, and to each other. I found that class and "race" divisions play a powerful role in both shaping young activists' sense of political selfhood in relation to the state and schooling, as well as in structuring the symbolic economy of youth activist subcultures themselves. Specifically, visible minority youth, Aboriginal youth, and youth from working-class histories often encountered the state and schooling as sites of class- and "race"-based injuries, where they perceived the "good citizen" to (still) be predicated on a white, middle-class norm, and apparatuses of "good citizenship" to follow liberal codes of community and political participation that served to shore up middle-class students' credentials within the new global economy. Young activists in general found school-based "citizenship education" to have little to do with their own sense of political priorities, even if some of the skills they gained could later be transferred to their activist practices.

Within youth activist subcultures themselves, the cultural context of liberalism and neoliberalism was felt through a structure of feeling that included extraordinary burdens of guilt and responsibility (particularly for women), the perceived requirement to be self-regulating and self-scrutinizing (the self-perfecting activist), and through subcultural codes of consumption that act to reduce political participation to such consumptive "choices" as buying fair trade organic coffee and avoiding Nike. Rituals of style further regulated young people's involvement in youth activist subcultures, in which a complex working-class/middle-class performance ("performing grunge") held sway as the dominant means through which to acquire the subcultural capital known as being "radical." Activism, as a cultural phenomenon, also takes a particular shape due to Canada's unique position within global power relations—that is, to be an "activist" in Canada often (although not always) implies that one is working on behalf of others, rather than for oneself. This is connected to the wider perception (and experience) of activism as largely a middle-class phenomenon—a perception that was supported by my field data documenting the class histories of my participants. The middle-class elements of youth activism, I would suggest, are connected intangibly to the wider cultural sphere of permissiveness for a particular kind of "good active citizen"—recognizable within middle-class codes of accomplishment—as well as to the family histories of middle-class activism from which many of the participants came. That is, although the "good citizen" as described earlier is generally not supposed to enter the realm of state-challenging activism, sometimes the "good citizen" who becomes engaged in community work via middle-class processes of desirable associations ends up moving into more oppositional activist practices (particularly if that person comes from a left-leaning family sympathetic to such a shift). That the class culture of youth activism is invariably middle class was felt most keenly by those who did not come from middle-class histories, as they relayed experiences of exclusion that carried the often invisible markers of class.

Class cultures in Canada are inseparable also from experiences of "race" and ethnicity, and how these regulate the complex processes of belonging. Participants from racialized communities often encountered subtle barriers to inclusion, which sometimes followed class lines, and at others occurred as an uncomfortable but necessary negotiation between family and cultural traditions and the practices of activism. In part because oppositional activist practices are represented as undesirable within the wider cultural sphere, the means of accessing these subcultures was often tightly associated with one's family history, and thus the habitus that one acquired. That such a family history was more commonly associated with the white middle classes also contributes to the shaping of a doxa of activism that remains largely white and middle class. While people from other histories did find their way into activist subcultures, they did so often with an associated sense of unease and structures of feeling that suggested they did not quite "fit," such that they found themselves on the edges of activist subcultures, if they were there at all.

This sense of unease was also shared, however, by people who might appear to fit within the modalities of white, middle-class activist experience, but who still encountered a sense of being "outside." Participants often pointed out that the rules of activist comportment are strict, and experienced what they perceived to be policing by those "authorized bearers" of "legitimate" activist credentials. I have identified the symbolic authority described by many of the research participants as manifesting through "performing grunge," whereby one must demonstrate a certain kind of "working-class comportment" (through taking low-income jobs, wearing used clothing, and living in cheap housing, for example), but do so from within a middle-class frame (be highly educated, be cognizant of relevant theorists, and be articulate about one's political ideologies). This "performance," which I identify as part of the broader function of class cultures, following Julie Bettie, is not carried out intentionally but takes place unconsciously, acting as a cultural mode through which the members of the subculture can identify "like" and "unlike." This particular class performance can unfortunately serve to mystify and indeed mask the often close alignments between middle-class assertions and practices and activism within Canada, and can further intensify the confusion and alienation experienced by those who come from working-class histories. While functioning to accrue a particular kind of subcultural capital to those who are able to play within its rules (often identified as being "radical"), such a performance does little, I would suggest, to further the important social justice work carried out by young activists. Instead, it can perversely serve to reinforce class- and "race"-based exclusions that mean young activists are sometimes left "preaching to the converted" at events and rallies.

That young people from outside of the constraints identified within this book have found their way into activist subcultures speaks both to the inherent fluidity of these barriers, and to the existence of a modality of involvement that manages to breach the walls of doxic (activist) "common sense." The capacity to become engaged in political struggles, even when one does not come from a family where the habitus to do so already exists, comes about, I suggest, through a process of interactional experiences that, following Lovell (2003) and McNay (2004), I have identified as "relational agency." Experienced by many young people as being "invited in," this theoretical articulation of the process of becoming politically active is able to acknowledge both the fact that there is an "in," and that the borders around activist subcultures cannot be entirely impenetrable. Thus, relational agency is able to capture both the fact of the constraints—theorized alongside Bourdieu as the existence of a specific activist habitus—and the means by which those who have not yet acquired this habitus can breach them. Although such breaching only seems to come about if one already carries a preexisting disposition that permits these relational connections to occur, this assessment of the mode by which young people can be "invited in" to activist practices highlights the importance of interactional processes over and above the individualized rational actor of liberal theory. It also recognizes the important role played by relationships, within a subculture that remains outside of the support and sanction of the mainstream, in enabling the difficult but necessary work of activist practices.

Political Possibilities in a High Modern Age, or: Where To From Here?

Much of this book was originally written in cafés across Toronto and Vancouver, fueled by innumerable decaf soy mochas. After pouring over its contents, thinking and rethinking my arguments, reviewing my data, rereading the theorists I had drawn upon, I would leave the café and reenter a world where pressing political issues screamed from posters flour-pasted onto telephone poles: "Free the Cuban Five!," "Stop the SPP!," "End Police Brutality!" Many of these events and posters, I knew, had been organized, designed, or posted by people I had interviewed, or people who know the people I had interviewed. Their urgency would press upon me, and I would wonder whether I was doing these movements, these people, and the larger struggle for social change a disservice through this research project. When so much political work remains to be done, how do I justify this close reading of youth activist subcultures, a reading that some will take as critique (in spite of all my protests to the contrary)? The best answer I can offer to this, to myself and to others, is that given by Pierre Bourdieu and Loïc Wacquant (1992) in their book entitled *An invitation to reflexive sociology*. In Wacquant's introduction to the book, where he provides a detailed overview of Bourdieu's theories, he writes: "In Bourdieu's eyes, the business of the sociologist is to denaturalize and to defatalize the social world, that is, to destroy the myths that cloak the exercise of power and the perpetuation of domination" (50). Bourdieu sees the purpose of his sociological work as being able to provide the tools and analysis by which social agents will be able to recognize and identify the structures within which they act, and thus work to shift those relations that prevent social and political emancipation. He sees this work as inherently political, because he does not understand the laws that the social world follows to be immutable:

> Though Bourdieu pictures the social world as highly structured, he disagrees with the idea that it evolves "according to immanent laws, which human actions are laughably impotent to modify" (Hirschmann, 1991: 72). For him, social laws are temporally and spatially bound regularities that hold as long as the institutional conditions that underpin them are allowed to endure. (52)

Thus Bourdieu and Wacquant argue that critical thinking, and empirical investigations like this one, are central to uncovering the power of the institutional and doxic influences on the social world. This project has sought to examine both of these elements, by a close investigation of the "cultural every day" of youth activist subcultural practices, as well as through an analysis of the wider institutional structures that shape the cultural sphere through which young people come to activism. It is thus my hope that the analysis that has come in the previous chapters will not depress people (as one reader commented it did to her on a previous draft), but will provide deeper insight into a particular set of social relations that are of pressing concern to anyone interested in the space available for contemporary democratic practices. In particular, it is my hope that those who wish to become involved in activist groups, but have experienced exclusions that result from submerged class and "race" harms, might be able to better identify these harms, and be thus emboldened in their own sense of legitimacy within activist circles. I also hope that those young people paralyzed by an overwhelming sense of (neo/liberal) guilt about their own capacity to act within the nation-state will find within these pages some sense of how their own personal struggles belong within a much wider cultural arena. As mentioned throughout in the form of parentheses and footnotes, my own developing analysis has had such an impact on myself; if anything, the opportunity to carry out this research has deepened my activist involvement (including, of course, the opportunity to meet several inspirational people who have helped draw me further in, thus strengthening my own relational ties that enable the enactment of my political agency). It has been my own emerging analysis that has allowed me to better recognize the class harms that I still encounter through certain activist circles, and those I have encountered in the past, to recognize the liberal guilt and neoliberal self-perfection demanded of young Canadians, and to be better able to separate my own emotional responses to these pressures from the requirement to act against the ongoing injustices that make up our social worlds. Thus, rather than this analysis leaving the reader with a sense of depression, it is my hope that this book will be an enlivening call to greater insight, particularly for those people resting on the margins of youth activist subcultures who wish to move deeper into the work that they feel is important.

It also offers, I hope, a more realistic assessment of the manner through which young people *can* be drawn further into activist practices, practices that I see as central to any properly functioning democratic public sphere. That is, I hope that my description of *relational agency* and the importance of such interactional structures for "inviting people in" to the alternative cultural worlds that make up activist lives will be a useful heuristic for those attempting to expand the circles of youth activist participation. Such an analysis is particularly important for shifting the emphasis away from the liberal individual and his or her private and solitary relationship with the state (exemplified through the act of voting), to a more embedded, community-based understanding of the process through which social change happens. Many activist organizations already understand this, and are busily creating networks and opportunities to bring other people into the life worlds of activist cultures. Such efforts will be most successful, I would suggest, when there exists a critical reflexivity within activist groups about the influences of class, "race," gender, liberalism, and neoliberalism in mediating who feels capable of accepting their invitation.

Finally, it is my hope that this book has helped to reveal one of the more troubling cultural phenomena happening at the moment in relation to young people and the idea of "citizenship." That citizenship has always been associated with those privileged few who have been at the center of political and social structures has more recently been mystified by the supposed "equality" that liberal democratic regimes are meant to uphold, and the concomitant call for universal citizenship participation. However, the "good citizen" of the contemporary moment continues to valorize a particular kind of middle-class enactment and set of assertions. While this enactment bears some minor resemblance to activist practices, the forms of community involvement called for are generally limited to apolitical acts of regulated charity that do little to challenge fundamental state structures of inequality. Further, the acts of "active citizenship" encouraged by today's curriculum are continually tempered by the caution to be "responsible" and "informed," qualities that may well be important but that function in this regard as a specific kind of neoliberal injunction within the context of a cultural sphere that includes media images of apparently out-of-control and hysterical activists. That citizenship education may have become another way to shift the burdens of state responsibility away from the government and toward individuals is one consequence of curricula that emphasize "responsibility" far beyond rights and entitlements (see also Kennelly & Llewellyn, in press). That it functions within a wider cultural sphere of suspicion toward youth activism (or any activism) means that the potential for much-needed oppositional engagement within the wider public sphere is substantially narrowed (see also Benhabib 1996). In addition, today's "good citizen," as experienced by participants within this project, continues to follow a white, middle-class imaginary, if not explicitly then at least in the felt experiences of growing up within a Canadian cultural sphere that has long been a place of white, middle-class aspirations.

Thus I hope that this book will also serve as a critical call to educators to scrutinize the forms of citizenship currently on offer through schooling. This is not a matter of political nicety; if we are indeed committed to a genuinely plural public sphere that challenges practices of oblivion (Arendt 1998; Curtis 1999), we must continually interrogate the forms of political education being directed toward young people. Given my findings, which suggest that the available space for oppositional practices (i.e., activist subcultures) have been influenced by liberalism and neoliberalism and histories of classism and racism such that they are now generally reserved for middle-class actors from activist families, it is my concern that the potential locust for diverse political opinions and public debate are being lost. Such a loss is grave indeed, and one that should cause concern for all educators and scholars of educational research.

Even as I put the finishing touches on this book, I am constantly confronted with the effects of the cultural space of Canadian citizenship and youth activism I have taken pains to paint throughout. One reminder comes in the form of a conversation in a café with someone I know through my community work in Vancouver, himself within the age range of my research participants. I am telling him about my work and he listens with interest; we then get into a conversation about his own search for activist organizations to work with, his sense of anger, despair, and futility at the current political situation, and his feeling of paralysis as to whether he will ultimately do the right thing. Another comes in the form of an e-mail from another young man, a friend of a friend, who has heard about my involvement with a youth activist organization, and wants to offer his assistance. He is in law school, and tempers his offer with a parenthetical comment wondering if we will accept a "sell-out lawyer" into our midst. Both of these recent conversations highlight for me that young people are constantly seeking out ways to commit to democratic projects designed to create social change. That they feel unable to do so, due to the relentless subjectification of our self-perfecting times (pace: will I do the right thing?) and the regulating impacts of wider cultural and subcultural scripts about what it means to be "an activist" (pace: they will never accept a "sell-out lawyer"), is an unacceptable situation in a time when renewed democratic engagement with the social issues of our time has perhaps never been so pressing. Ongoing scrutiny of both the microsociological components of everyday political cultures and practices, combined with the insights provided through a hermeneutic *detour* through the historical, social, and political contexts that partially constitute the present, is part of the formula for generating a critical awareness of the elements that will promote a more plural and democratic public sphere. It is my hope that this book can contribute, in some small way, to an ongoing and necessary dialogue about the nature and means through which democracy and justice can be continually expanded.

Appendix: Research Methods

> What happens if we understand the raw materials of everyday lived cultures as if they were living art forms?
> —Willis 2000, ix

The aim of this appendix is to illuminate the methodological, theoretical, and pragmatic questions and dilemmas that went into the process of "gathering data." The means by which such processes are undertaken within a research project are often mystified, disguised by polished prose and the assured tone of academic discourse. The reality is that social research—indeed, *all* research—is messy, involving contradictions, problems, and uncertainties. In other words, social research is forever interlaced with the problematic of human relating. This appendix attempts to lay bare some of these issues, with as much reflexivity as possible. The appendix is also where I have provided a detailed description of the manner in which I categorized participants in terms of class and "race"/ethnicity. This in itself is a prime example of the messiness inherent to social research, and serves as a glimpse into the manner in which one researcher has attempted to address the related dilemmas.

Phenomenology, Ethnography, Culture

This research project has been informed by a phenomenological methodology and theoretical frame. Phenomenology is concerned with how people come to understand their own social and cultural worlds—or, how they develop and account for their common-sense knowledge about the world (Dillabough et al. 2005; see also Dillabough & Kennelly 2010). As Ricoeur (1998) states, "the most fundamental phenomenological presupposition of a philosophy of interpretation is that every question concerning any sort of 'being' [*étant*] is a question about the meaning of that 'being'" (114). As such, phenomenology is a natural epistemological home for an ethnographic study. Willis (2000) situates ethnography as the methodological approach that can encounter and record the widest range of individual sense-making practices in a tradition that draws strongly upon a concern with the cultural everyday, as advocated by Raymond Williams (1989). Such an approach is also indebted to hermeneutic insights about the interpretive nature of the social world, and the ways in which individuals try to articulate, express, and comprehend their experiences and that of those around them. As Paul Ricoeur (1998) explains, "each society has created its own medium of understanding by creating the social and cultural worlds in which it understands itself" (52). This means that the process of inquiry through which I come to my interpretations of my research participants' lives is forever mediated by our shared existence within society and culture, which both provides insight into and generates confusion about the meanings contained therein. In other words, an "ethnographic imagination," as called for by Willis (2000), is necessary to interpret the meanings and life worlds of those with whom I research. He writes: "Of fundamental importance to the ethnographic imagination is comprehending creativities of the everyday as indissolubly connected to, dialectically and intrinsically, wider social structures, structural relations and structurally provided conditions of existence" (34). The "cultural" is therefore not seen as separate from the "structural," but neither is it understood as standing in a straightforward relationship with it; rather, it is a location through which the structural can be glimpsed, as can the modes of refusal, resistance, or co-optation taken up by people living within that cultural milieu.

    Reflexivity is central to a hermeneutic and phenomenological approach. It is also consistent with the critical, feminist, and postcolonial methodological approaches that have influenced my work (Britzman 1995; Lather 2001; Smith 1999). I understand reflexivity as both an intentional practice designed to respond to the concerns of critical, feminist, and postcolonial scholars about the importance of revealing one's own position in the always ethically troubling process of social research, and also as an integral component of the methodological process that I am employing. In *An invitation to reflexive sociology* (1992), Bourdieu and Wacquant describe the role of reflexivity to be much more than a simple "placing" of the researcher within social relations. Rather they posit reflexivity as something that must move beyond social relations toward an understanding of how the researcher's position, *as researcher*, influences the interpretation of the data. DeSales Turner (2003) further points out that a hermeneutic methodology requires one to present information to a reader regarding one's own understanding of the social phenomena at hand such that the reader can assess the truth content for himself or herself. Ricoeur also emphasized that we can never have a view from nowhere; our situated selves are not only physically located, but also "socially, culturally and politically situated and contingent" (Langdridge 2004, 252). Willis (2000) writes, "I have long argued for a form of reflexivity, emphasizing the importance of maintaining a sense of the investigator's history, subjectivity and theoretical positioning as a vital resource for the understanding of, and respect for, those under study" (113). Consequently, I interspersed the book with references to my own situated self, in order to highlight how I, as researcher, was constantly a part of the research process. As these excerpts revealed, my own embodiment played an integral role in the research, whether it was due to my appearance (and what this meant for how others responded to me) or my emotions (and how this impacted on my capacity to carry out elements of the research). Both of these elements were inseparable from the research process; as a result, each find their way into the data analysis, where it seems relevant to the discussion at hand.

The balance, as articulated by Fine et al. (2003), is always between the need for a critical assessment and explication of the relationship between those asking the questions and those who are answering them, and the problem of what Patricia Clough has called a "compulsive extroversion of interiority" (as cited in Fine et al. 2003, 170). That is, reflexivity must walk a fine line between positioning oneself within the research, and making the entire project about the researcher. With this in mind, I have worked to articulate my presence within the research when it seemed particularly relevant. In data analysis, this means drawing upon my own emotional responses and embodied presence as one means by which to better articulate and describe the arguments that I am making.

One of the most important—and most difficult—locations through which I approached this research was as a member of some of the youth activist communities from which I drew participants. Responding in part to Bennett's (2002) call for a more critical evaluation of the use of "insider knowledge" as a methodological tool in youth research, I would suggest that it was my role as both an "insider" and an "outsider" within this research process that allowed me to (at least partially) encounter and experience the "cultural every day" of youth activist communities. As a long time volunteer with and board member of a well-known youth-driven social justice organization in Vancouver, I approached my research from the tenuous position of being both "inside" of the youth activist communities that I was researching, and—as a slightly older person and doctoral student (at the time of data collection)—also as an "outsider" to these communities. This position powerfully structured the access that I was able to negotiate with youth activists, some of whom would otherwise have been undoubtedly hesitant to engage in a research project. Indeed, the greatest success that I found in recruiting participants was through my contacts; almost every attempt that I made to access youth activists through impersonal modes (such as list serves or postering) drew no response. This was not particularly surprising; as a research project on what Paul Willis (2000) calls "social connection" (xvi), having a personal relationship with research participants became a necessary means through which to gain some partial access to their deeper social and cultural worlds. Also not surprising was that it was with the people with whom I had a prior connection that I was generally able to go the farthest; these were the people most likely to invite me to their activist events, who were the most open and forthcoming in their interviews, and who were most helpful in connecting me with other potential participants. Such generosity, built on the trust established through our prior collaborations, became a sensitive sticking point for me as I began to analyze the data and develop my theoretical arguments. Specifically, the ethical dilemma became how to accurately represent the incredible energy, commitment, and integrity of these individuals, while simultaneously critiquing the forms of practice that I argue limit the participation of young people in activist subcultures along class and "race" lines. Similarly to Julie Bettie (2003), who notes the likelihood that her middle-class participants felt "betrayed" because of her "emotional allegiance...to working class girls" (26), my own work may be seen by some of my middle-class participants as unfairly critical of them and their lives.

Beyond giving me access to research participants, my prior and ongoing engagement in youth activist communities *as an activist* posed specific opportunities and dilemmas throughout the research process. Because of the relationships that I developed through meeting activists from across the country, and because of our shared interests in social change, I became involved in several new activist projects, and was invited to speak at public forums about my research and my own community work. The issue that this raised for me was where to draw the line between being a "researcher" and being simply there as the person that I am, as someone who is involved with activist, lefty and queer circles[1] across all three cities where I carried out this research. I would often end up at events where I happened to meet some of my research participants, because of our mutual interests and involvement. It would become tempting at that point to pull out my notebook and begin making ethnographic observations, particularly when situations played out that were directly related to my research interests. However, I ultimately chose to limit my ethnographic note-taking only to the events where I had been specifically invited by a participant *as* a researcher, in this way trying to respect both my own need for rest from the research, as well as the privacy of my research participants. Nonetheless, my participation in such events, throughout and prior to the research project, cannot help but become the backdrop of my comprehension of youth activist communities. Is it ever possible to actually "turn off" the inner researcher? While any field notes cited throughout this book come from situations in which I was explicitly there as a researcher, nonetheless my sense of the community, what might be called my aesthetic intuition about activist subcultures, is also inevitably drawn from this larger context of experiences.

Given this, I see my position as both an insider and an outsider (inasmuch as I could be either of these things at any one time) to this research process as being an integral aspect of my methodology and highly consistent with the cultural ethnographic approach that I described earlier. How better to get inside the skin of a subculture than to be involved in it already? This of course poses specific and important challenges: one such being my inner battle, as outlined earlier, with a sense of betrayal of the remarkable people who participated in this project. The other challenge, difficult in different ways, was to achieve the analytical distance necessary to even come to such a critique in the first place. The people reflected within this book are *my people*, or closely resemble the people with whom I have come to my own sense of identity. Nonetheless, I recognize within them some of the same struggles for recognition that I also have engaged with in my activist life world. Coming as I do from a single-parent family and a working-class/working-poor background, I am intensely empathetic with the participant who explained the following to me:

> *Karen*: I just always feel like I have this other identity, like I don't really have the same sort of sense, because my family is so, in some ways, not traditional that...you kind of feel like you have a secret identity. And it's weird because people kind of expect like because you're so, like, people are like "you're so well-adjusted" that they just expect this kind of thing.

My struggle, then, was to separate myself from my own desire to belong within the activist circles so similar to the ones in which I came to adulthood, and begin to recognize the patterns of classed and raced behavior that characterize these communities. I had to put aside my admiration and (I must also admit) my envy, and try to attain enough analytical distance to assess the ways in which these dynamics were playing out. This was never easy, and I likely achieved it in only partial ways.

Another difficult question that plagued me throughout this research process has been that of "why?" Why am I doing this research? Who will it benefit? Who will it harm? This was not only an internal question; I occasionally received such challenges from others, especially from those involved in activist circles. One colleague questioned whether my work might be used by the state to assist them in their repression of activism. I had a lengthy e-mail exchange with a participant who questioned whether a research project on activism was necessary, or whether academics ought to be focusing instead on the problems created by social inequalities within the state (I considered it a minor affirmation of my reasoning when he ultimately agreed to do an interview with me, after I offered a detailed e-mail explanation of my rationale). At an activist meeting, I overheard another academic who has also done research on activism in the past say that she was switching her research focus toward policing, because activists did not need to be studied any more.

My response to this line of questioning, both internal and external, is twofold. First of all, as discussed in the opening chapter, while this study is certainly about youth activist subcultures, the larger framing context is the global influence of neoliberalism on youth cultures and youth political participation, with a specific focus on the current case study of the Canadian nation-state. Thus, this project is at least as much about the cultural sphere of the Canadian state, and its modes of representing and reinforcing the idea of the "good citizen," as it is about activism. Second, following Paul Willis (2000), I hope that this project will contribute to "the responsible provision of possible materials towards the reflexivity of social agents themselves" (149). That is, through documenting the aspects of class- and "race"-based harms occurring within youth activist subcultures, I hope to provide some small catalyst for reflexivity and change within these subcultures. Loïc Wacquant (2004) notes that critical thought may be the only means by which to dissolve doxa, where doxa represents the social norms of specific fields of interaction; I hope that this critical intervention will permit the dissolution of some of the problematic elements of the doxa of youth activist subcultures, or at least provide some tools for reflexivity for those who read this book.

At the least, it has provided me with some of the requisite analytical tools to bring to my own activist practices; this is having an influence within my own small sphere of community work, as I engage in ongoing conversations about how to lessen the class- and "race"-based exclusions within the groups with which I work, and about the emotional and personal effects of growing up under the shadow of neoliberalism.

In order to facilitate the latter process, I have attempted to make both myself and my research as accessible as possible throughout and after the research period. In addition to being as transparent as I was able to be about my developing analysis within interviews, I also made a point of inviting participants to an early academic presentation of this research in Toronto; in Vancouver, I organized a special session for community youth activist organizations, to which I also invited participants. I was also invited by one of the community organizations with which I am involved to present my research findings, in an accessible format, as part of a "training program" for young people interested in becoming involved in social justice or activist work. Once I had completed the first draft of the then dissertation, I sent it to all participants who were interested and encouraged them to provide me with their thoughts or feedback. I invited all participants and other local youth activist organizations to attend my final PhD defense in Vancouver. Finally, I have distributed all articles produced from this research to my participants, as well as to other relevant organizations. Ensuring that my research will be read or heard by the participants themselves and by other youth activists is one effective way of ensuring my own reflexivity, in that it forces me to be certain that my claims are accurate and defensible, beyond the requirements given those qualities by academic discipline. In many ways, I think this kind of participant feedback might be a more rigorous peer review process than that instituted within academia itself; if my research does not in some way resonate with the people about whom it is written, then I have done something wrong indeed. This is not to say that individual participants will have the final say over the product I create; the work is mine, and necessarily filtered through my specific set of experiences, perspectives, and interests. However, an effective ethnography ought to, at the least, make sense to the people who are living it. As Paul Willis (2000) notes, "no ethnographer should ever say, 'This is how it is,' or 'I know better than you do about your life.' The point at issue is whether understanding and human empathy are increased or not" (120).

Finally, one other major ethical dilemma for me throughout, which is true for any research project but is perhaps more apparent for a project informed by hermeneutics and phenomenology, is the question of "writing up" the results. Specifically, the issue becomes how to do this in a way that even comes close to resembling the social and cultural worlds that were the subject of this study. As Ricoeur (1998) notes, "to interpret is to render near what is far... The text is, *par excellence,* the basis for communication in and through distance" (111). Thus the hermeneutic process is inevitably concerned with textual representation, whether that "text" be written or spoken. The act of interpretation always requires the application of words to a situation outside of oneself—through what Ricoeur (1998) calls distanciation. That textual representation is necessary to the hermeneutic and phenomenological project does not clarify the best means by which to create such representations, however. As Paul Willis (2000) writes,

> Especially when it is trying to be scientific, linguistic communication usually flattens rather than evokes phenomena, so artifice to the limits of language is sometimes necessary. Written art is needed to re-create living art. Art reproducing art!... This can be the *only* means of presenting the "rough ground" on which agents live and move, showing the complexity of lived relations and forms for which words and theories do not yet exist, but which somehow, in practice, and in the practical relations of the field, connect up some of the important elements that interest the researcher. (118; emphasis in the original)

While I am certain that my attempts at representation within these pages are not even roughly comparable to art, I am compelled by Willis' encouragement to make use of the creative edges of language in order to best represent the complex cultural worlds of the young people who I encountered in this research. In particular, his injunction helps to highlight the ways in which language can be used to foreclose possibilities, "flatten[ing] rather than evok[ing] phenomena." Specifically, I am concerned that by committing my analysis to the written page it acquires a problematic authority and rigidity—particularly once it is published in book format—that does not do justice to the multiple meanings that have eluded these pages. Without a great deal of provisos and apologies, which can quickly become distracting, it is easy for a piece of writing to stand in as a completed work, as if it has been able to capture all of the complexities, messiness, and uncertainty that make up social and cultural reality. While the possibility for creative expression and multilingual articulation provided by ethnography helps forestall this somewhat, I am aware that even my own theories look weightier to me once they are on the page. What I want to note here, then, is the fact that this written document, with its associated theories and the tiny percentage of ethnographic data that I was able to incorporate out of thousands of pages of transcripts, field notes, and visual representations, is necessarily partial, incomplete, and open to reinterpretation. I do not write this in the spirit of unlimited and infinite forms of indeterminacy—I believe that there are social, material, and cultural realities that can be more or less captured as a system of meaning, through research and careful representation. But a text such as this one will never include everything, nor should that be the task to which it aspires.

The Details: Methods and Participants

Each participant's involvement in the research project began with a semistructured interview. While some of the interviews proceeded more or less as documented within the protocol and lasted about two hours, others ranged back and forth across topics, incorporating sidetracks and non-sequiters, and lasted up to four hours. This had everything to do with the style of the interviewee, as I endeavored to follow their lead and allow the interview to take the shape with which they were most comfortable. I often found that the interviews created a sense of intimacy, particularly noticeable when I was interviewing someone with whom I had no prior history. This intimacy was both welcome and troubling, as I recognized it to be one-sided—I interpreted the intimacy as being created because of the personal details they had just shared with me, but of course I had shared very little of myself in return. I was happy to share pieces of my own story when the opportunity arose, or when I was asked—indeed, I felt an ethical obligation to do so, due to this intimacy I had uneasily noticed developing—but often the interviews ended without a two-way exchange. Many participants remarked that they enjoyed the interview, appreciating the opportunity to speak at length about themselves and to work through some of their thoughts on activism, citizenship, and democracy. Participants also consistently apologized for talking too much, reflective perhaps of the (Canadian?) taboo associated with "dominating" a conversation, particularly with strangers.

At the end of the interview, I would inform them of the other two stages of the research and invite their participation in each, as they saw fit. The second stage was a shadowing process, whereby I would attend anything that they felt related to their activist practice, and to which they felt comfortable inviting me. The result was that I attended an array of events and activities, including, but not limited to, an arts-based urban youth project, a university class, a play, a conference, various protests, a fundraising cabaret, various public forums, and multiple activist planning meetings. This shadowing process was the means whereby I gathered ethnographic observations, standing in for the fact that there is no central gathering place through which I could observe youth activist cultures [such as the standard gathering places of youth used by other ethnographers, including schools (e.g., Bettie 2003; Willis 1977) or music clubs (e.g., Thornton 1996)].

The third stage of the data collection was a focus group, held in each city near the end of my research time there. During the two-hour focus group, I engaged participants in an arts-based process (Harper 1998). This was one of the means through which the visual and the symbolic were engaged, as a way to both trigger further dialogue, as well as to access submerged representations, images, and ideas that were not readily accessible through the interview or participant-observation format.

For example, participants jointly created an image of the "perfect activist"; the process for this involved a large piece of paper with a vaguely person-shaped blob already drawn on it, to which they added symbols and characteristics that they associated with the idea of the "perfect activist." The images that were created represented both the pressures felt by young activists from each other, as well as broader media representations, circulating rhetoric within popular culture, and the ideals that participants themselves hold central to activism. The creation of these images provoked laughter, commiseration, disagreement, and in-depth conversations. In this manner, the visual and symbolic, while ultimately not becoming a data source, functioned as a fruitful creative prompt through which participants could access and express some of the stickier aspects of their complex location as "activists" (for a related methodological approach using drama, see Gallagher 2007).

The number of participants at each research site was partially determined by my own physical proximity to each city. Whereas the Vancouver and Toronto fieldwork were carried out while I lived in each city, I traveled to and from Montreal while living in Toronto in order to interview activists there. This necessarily limited the number of people I could reasonably interview, and also curbed my capacity to shadow Montreal participants to the same extent as I could with those living in Vancouver and Toronto. I spent six months in Vancouver and another six in Toronto; while in Toronto, I made four trips to Montreal, visits that varied in length from one night to one week. Within the Vancouver site, I carried out interviews with sixteen participants between the ages of seventeen and twenty-nine; in Toronto, I interviewed twelve participants between the ages of thirteen and twenty-nine; and in Montreal, I interviewed ten participants between the ages of twenty and twenty-seven. I had the opportunity to shadow almost all of the participants for at least one activist event; some participants I spent more time with than others, depending on their availability and interest. There were also additional participants in two of the three focus groups; in Vancouver, two additional people who did not take part in the rest of the project participated in the focus group, and in Toronto, one additional person participated. Thus, the total number of young people who participated across all aspects of the project in the three cities totaled forty-one. The average age of all participants was twenty-three; of all the participants interviewed, twenty-two were female, and sixteen were male (including one transgendered man).

I chose to focus on young people involved in forms of activism that I viewed as directly contesting the state. In my mind, this encompassed antiglobalization, antipoverty, anticolonialism, and antiwar activism—four interlocking webs of engagement, which, in my experience, drew many of the same people to their organizing meetings. As noted earlier, I generally found participants through my own contacts and through word-of-mouth. Beginning in Vancouver, I set up interviews with a few people I had collaborated with on other projects, and they referred me to other people, who then referred me to still others, and so on (also known as snowballing). Once I moved to Toronto, I drew on contacts I still had there from when I had lived in that city five years before. I also called upon my Vancouver participants to connect me with anyone they might know, finding that many of the activist networks stretched across the country.[2] In all three cities, I contacted local activist and social justice organizations who sent out my call through their list serves. This was rarely directly successful, although it did function to get my name and project out into the activist ether, so that when someone was directly referred by another participant, she or he might have previously heard about the project, which seemed to increase my legitimacy as someone who was "in the know."

Class Histories, Ethnic Identities

I began this research project without a particular focus on social class, instead curious about how youth activists understood citizenship and democracy and used these concepts within their practices. However, after only a few interviews it became clear to me that class played a more powerful mediating role within youth activism than I had previously considered. Even so, I was surprised when I sat down to compile the class histories of the thirty-eight participants for whom I had this data (excluding those who only took part in the focus groups) to find that the majority of them came from middle- or upper middle-class family backgrounds. I include this information here, alongside a description of how I analyzed the data in this case, in order to provide the reader with some further context through which to understand the analysis contained throughout the book. I also discuss, in broad terms, the ethnicity of the participants in the following paragraphs.

Table A.1 categorizes the class histories of my research participants. I developed these categories based on interview data in which I queried participants about parental occupation and higher education, as well as their own access to higher education. There is a specific ethical issue associated with this, because it meant that I was interpreting participants' class history, rather than allowing them to locate themselves.[3] Indeed, one participant who attended an early presentation of this research said to me afterward, "I don't remember talking about class!"—much to my relief, she seemed amused rather than upset that I had taken the analysis in this direction. My rationale for treating class in this way was my sense that asking people to describe their family history would provide a richer framework within which to understand their class locations, as well as other relevant aspects of their activist development. This seemed a better starting point than a simple question such as "what class did you grow up in?". This, I thought, would neither elicit such rich data nor necessarily provide an accurate account, given the

Table A.1 Class location by parental occupational history ($N = 38$)

Business/professional class (BPC) = 18 (47%)[a]
Middle class = 11 (29%)[b]
Immigrant middle class to working class = 5 (13%)[c]
Working class = 4 (11%)

[a] Professions included within the BPC: lawyer, university or college professor, dentist, religious leader, advertising consultant, dancer/started dance company, accountant, stockbroker, animal behavioralist, owner of mid-to-large business, chemist, and stock exchange trader.
[b] Professions included within middle class: teacher, scientist (not at university), government employee, writer, filmmaker, social worker, motel manager, salesman, and owner of small business.
[c] Professions included in immigrant middle class to working class and working class: factory worker, trucking, sales (telephone), laborer, secretary, physiotherapist's assistant, hairdresser, and taxi driver.

subjective nature of class affiliations, and how the pervasive belief in the universality of middle classness holds sway within a country such as Canada (i.e., both those from poor or working-class histories and those from highly affluent families will identify themselves as "middle class").

In order to turn this rich data into class categories, I drew in part on the typology offered by Sherry Ortner (2003), in which she specified the class location of her research participants based on family occupational history. In her ethnography of graduates from her own high-school class of 1958, she divided her participants into three class categories, based on the occupation of the primary breadwinner within the family: business/professional class (BPC), middle class, and working class (30). Within her categories, the BPC generally included doctors, lawyers, and owners of larger businesses; the middle class included teachers, bookkeepers, and owners of small businesses; and the working class included manual laborers and tradespeople. While noting that occupational history has been controversial within academic studies as an indicator of class, she suggests that "the mixture of cultural factors (prestige notions about different kinds of work) and Marxist assumptions (about the importance of position within a mode of production) renders occupation a reasonable mode of defining and ordering class positions" (ibid.). She also notes, however, that other criteria such as education, income, and lifestyle can shape one's subjective perception of both one's own and others' class position. I would further add that immigration history plays an important role in shaping class, especially within the context of a state such as Canada that brings in skilled labor to make up for labor shortages without recognizing credentials from other countries (particularly "Third World" or "developing" countries; Abu-Laban 1998).

Given these criteria, I have created a modified set of categories to describe the class history of my participants, although recognizing that such categories are not strictly bound by class. I have followed Ortner in her categorization of BPC, middle class, and working class, but have added the category "immigrant middle class to working class" to highlight the common situation of immigrant families having come from middle-class histories in their countries of origin, but accessing only working-class jobs once they reach Canada. Given that the majority of my participants were either still living at home, or had just recently left their parents' home, I think it is legitimate to categorize their class history based on parental occupation, in consideration of the pivotal role this would have played in shaping their own access to both material and cultural capital. However, "class" is not always this neatly defined, and a table such as this is not adequate for reflecting such complexity. For example, one participant began life in a wealthy family with an entrepreneurial father who later left home. The participant and his mother struggled to make ends meet until the mother acquired further training and became a stock promoter, thus able to again bring in a high income. Within the typology I have created, I categorized this participant within the business-professional class (BPC) category, but obviously this does not capture his complex class history. Another issue with respect to taking parental occupational history as the primary marker of class is that often one parent's work would be classified within one category, and the other's in another (a lawyer married to a legal secretary, for example). In those cases, I classified participants within the higher class location, which generally seemed consistent with participants' reported experiences of growing up and the types of opportunities they had (educational and extracurricular). Finally, the question of which professions belong in which categories is a difficult one, and was troubling to Ortner (2003) as well. On this issue, she writes,

> Readers will surely differ regarding which occupations should go in which class locations. Is a musician, or a pharmacist, or a rabbi really a member of the BPC? There is no final answer, because it is a cultural system on which different people have different readings. I have tried to approximate what I take to be the standard or dominant view. (31)

Similar to Ortner, I have attempted to classify professions following both her typology (thus placing imam and owner of dance company in the BPC, for example), as well as my own sense of the broader context of each individual's story (thus there is a "salesman" in the middle-class category, but a person who does telephone sales in the working-class category). That class is both aligned with occupational histories and much messier than that is an indisputable fact of social research. Despite these complexities, the aggregate results of the class histories of my thirty-eight participants across three provinces is overwhelmingly middle and business/professional class.

Noteworthy is that even those few participants who came from a working-class or immigrant-middle-class-to-working-class history have since made a class shift, either by attending institutions of higher education or, in one case, through comparable professional achievements that included holding political office and starting a not-for-profit organization.

Questions about family history also elicited rich data about participants' national, ethnic, and cultural histories. Rather than breaking these down along lines of specific national, ethnic, or cultural identities (of which there would often be only one participant per category), I have divided participants into two categories that are broadly similar to the forms of "short-hand" used within the wider Canadian culture, and within youth activist communities themselves: that is, I have divided my participants into those who are "white" and those who are "visible minority or Aboriginal." Of the forty-one participants who took part in this research project, they can be over-simplistically described as follows: white: 27; visible minority or Aboriginal: 14. This characterization, of course, vastly oversimplifies the complex racial, class, and migration histories of participants. For example, it lumps together "white" participants whose families migrated from Britain several generations ago with "white" participants whose parents arrived recently from impoverished countries in Eastern Europe. Similarly, it collapses differences of class, culture, and identity associated with coming from an affluent family born in Hong Kong versus a refugee family from Africa or South America. Nonetheless, the appearance of participants as white or as visible minority or Aboriginal often mediated their experiences of belonging and citizenship within Canada (for reasons addressed throughout the book). Noteworthy is that class histories cannot be easily mapped onto this categorization of "race"/ethnicity: in other words, there were both middle-class and working-class participants in both groups.

Notes

Introduction: "Citizen Youth" in the Twenty-first Century

1. The disparity between youth who are able to find success within Canada and those who are not can be seen perhaps most starkly in statistics associated with youth incarceration—of which Canada has one of the highest rates in the world, higher even than the United States. For example, of youth who are incarcerated, 33 percent are Aboriginal, even though Aboriginal youth comprise only 5 percent of the population (Dean 2005). Another example of this disparity can be found in a study of Canadian young adults (ages twenty to twenty-four) with low levels of education; the study found that young people who had not completed high school were 22 percent less likely to be employed than their peers who had a high-school or trade vocational diploma, and 28 percent less likely to be employed than their peers with a postsecondary education. The study noted that this gap was higher than that for many other OECD countries (de Broucker 2005). A recently released report card on child poverty in Canada (Campaign 2000, 2007) notes that child poverty rates are the same today as they were in 1989, despite a 50 percent real increase in the size of the economy over that period.
2. For a detailed discussion of the effects of neoliberalism at the municipal level across two of the three cities discussed here (Toronto and Vancouver), see Fanelli and Paulson (2010).

1 Understanding Youth Political Engagement: Youth Citizenship as Governance

1. Stasiulis (2002) gives the example of the Ontario Ministry of Education appointing a supervisor to take over the Ottawa-Carleton

school board, "because the board's trustees had refused to pass a budget doing away with a $23 million deficit on the grounds that further cuts would irreparably damage the Ottawa educational system" (527).
2. John Bynner (1997) also points out that some young people never experience full inclusion in citizenship, e.g., if they are marginalized by disability or by growing up in care.

2 Constructing the Good Youth Citizen: A History of the Present

1. The history of education in Canada, like any genealogical exploration, is a topic of some disagreement and represents an ever-evolving body of scholarship. For example, Anthony Di Mascio (2010) traces the evolution of academic consensus on the institution of public schooling in Canada, noting the shifting focus of academic studies since the latter half of the nineteenth century. Where earlier generations of scholarship emphasized the contributions of "great men" (in Canada, these included Egerton Ryerson and John Strachan), who designed a universal education system with the intention of promoting equality, scholars in the 1960s and 1970s began to critique these "great men" as socially conservative "school promoters" involved in the "construction of a school system that taught the values of an emerging urban and middle class" (35).
2. There are other provinces in Canada, of course, each with their own history of schooling, complete with local conflicts and tensions. I focus on Ontario, Quebec, and British Columbia, to the extent that I focus on any specific provinces within this chapter, because these were the three provinces in which I carried out the ethnography.
3. Janet Siltanen (2002) points out that such an idealized welfare state was never actually fully realized within Canada, even at the apex of social citizenship.
4. The results of my analysis in brief: Across the three curricular documents combined, of ninety-nine references to being "responsible," almost a third (twenty-eight) were directly connected to citizenship, while almost half (forty-five) were paired with "rights." With a more detailed analysis of the BC document (British Columbia Ministry of Education 2005), I discovered that out of one hundred occurrences of the words "citizen" and "citizenship," thirty-eight were preceded by "active" (e.g., "active citizenship"); thirteen were

paired with "responsible," "duty," or "ethical behaviour"; five were linked to "informed"; eleven were preceded by "informed" (e.g., "informed citizenship"); and fourteen were linked to "responsible" (e.g., "responsible citizenship"). For a more detailed description of the process used and the findings for two of these provinces, see Kennelly & Llewellyn (in press).
5. My own emotional journey through this research may be relevant here, as I found my relationship to activism shifting while I carried out this project. Always involved with activist groups in Vancouver, my research in Toronto and Montreal led me to further engagement with a variety of activist projects across the country. If anything, my own developing analysis of the complicity of the nation-state in constructing the "good (compliant) citizen," and my insights about the classed, gendered, and racialized nature of activism within this context, permitted me to deepen my involvement. For example, I was more able to discern feelings of guilt and responsibility as remnants of Canadian liberalism versus the urge to participate in activist projects in order to create much-needed change. I was also more able to identify the forms of class harm I had previously encountered, and encountered again; in so identifying them, I was able to distance myself from the emotional response of "not belonging" and recognize the ways in which class (in my case) played out in interactions with other activists. I also gained new insights into the ways in which I perpetuated class and "race" harms in my interactions with others, and felt more capable of scrutinizing my own behaviors for these hidden consequences.

3 Good Citizen/Bad Activist: The Cultural Role of the State in Youth Political Participation

1. All names of research participants within the book are pseudonyms.
2. The Pope Squat was a four-month occupation of an abandoned building in Toronto, organized by the Ontario Coalition Against Poverty in order to bring attention to the ongoing homelessness crisis in Ontario (Give Us The Keys 2006). For a detailed archive of newspaper articles and news releases about the Pope Squat, see http://www.ocap.ca/ocapnews/pope_squat.html.
3. This aspect of activist subcultures will be elaborated in greater detail in chapter four, within the section entitled 'Regimes of symbolic authorization: consumption, activism, identity' (99).

4. The arguments in this section are elaborated on and expanded in an article recently published by with the *British Journal of Criminology* (Kennelly, 2011).

4 Class Exclusions, Racialized Identities: The Symbolic Economy of Youth Activism

1. For a detailed description of the class histories and ethnic identities of participants, see appendix (155ff).
2. By "left-leaning," I mean the constellation of political practices and beliefs that are generally associated with the political left in Canada. These generally include being supportive of unions, critical of the erosion of the social safety net, opposed to war, supportive of same-sex rights and abortion, and pro-environment.
3. Because of the semistructured nature of the interviews, not every interview contained references to parental political beliefs.
4. Throughout the book, I use "visible minority" and "people of color" interchangeably. I recognize that each term has its own issues and restrictions, and use them interchangeably in partial recognition of this complex social reality, wrought from fraught histories of Canadian racism. DePass and Qureshi (2002), for example, note their own preference for the term "people of colour" "because it is a self-selected term for self-definition" (177). "Visible minority" maintains focus on the context of Canada as a white-dominant society in which one's "invisibility" is often concurrent with "whiteness" (see Brand 1994).
5. There are important distinctions between the experiences of Aboriginal peoples within Canada and those of ethnic minority and racialized individuals, though they may share encounters with racism and class-based subordination within a white-dominant society. By grouping them together here, I do not mean to suggest that the issues are continuous or indistinct.
6. To expand upon this point slightly: Hannah Arendt (1998) famously argued that human rights are *not*, in fact, universal, inasmuch as they require state recognition and protection in order to be fulfilled. Giorgio Agamben (1998) builds on this idea when he refers to the *state of exception* that exists in refugee camps and at airports or borders—i.e., one's rights are not protected within these interstate sites, due to the absence of a protective, rights-enforcing nation-state. The point I am trying to make here is that there is an important connection to be made between one's *belonging* to a state and one's sense of entitlement to protection from

within that state (and not only one's own sense of entitlement, but the way in which one is treated by others, e.g., the gatekeepers who might prevent one from accessing full citizenship rights through the welfare state).

7. At another point within the interview, Karen shares her mother's struggle to care for her brother, who was dying of cancer. Her mother left her job in order to nurse him, and, in the face of cuts to pharmaceutical supports and the health care system during the reign of Mike Harris's Conservatives within Ontario, was unable to afford the expensive drugs that would have eased his pain during this difficult period. Given such a context, the desire of Karen's parents that she "concentrate on [her]self" takes on heightened meaning and material relevance within a neoliberal era.

8. From *An invitation to reflexive sociology*: "Symbolic violence, to put it as tersely and simply as possible, is the *violence which is exercised upon a social agent with his or her complicity*...This is why the analysis of the doxic acceptance of the world, due to the immediate agreement of objective structures and cognitive structures, is the true foundation of a realistic theory of domination and politics. Of all forms of 'hidden persuasion,' the most implacable is the one exerted, quite simply, by the *order of things*" (Bourdieu and Wacquant 1992, 167–168; italics in the original). From *Pascalian meditations*: "[O]ne has to take account of the fact that the automatic effects of the conditionings imposed by the conditions of existence are added to by the directly educative interventions of the family, the peer group and the agents of the educational system (assessments, advice, injunctions, recommendations), which expressly aim to favor the adjustment of aspirations to objective chances, needs to possibilities, the anticipation and acceptance of the limits, both visible and invisible, explicit and tacit. By discouraging aspirations oriented to unattainable goals, which are thereby defined as illegitimate pretensions, these calls to order tend to underline or anticipate the sanctions of necessity and to orientate aspirations towards more realistic goals, more compatible with the chances inscribed in the position occupied" (Bourdieu 1997, 217).

9. In a recent popular book entitled *The rebel sell: why the culture can't be jammed* (2004), Canadian academics Joseph Heath and Andrew Potter identify some similar themes to those I have noted within this chapter, naming the group and their actions "counter-culture rebels," and chastising them for their political futility. However, unlike Heath and Potter, my argument is that

class, race, and histories of liberalism/neoliberalism cannot be separated from an analysis of why some young people take up activist practices and others do not. Rather than incorporating a cultural and sociological analysis into their assessment, Heath and Potter simply rebuke young people for being so politically foolish. (Particularly irksome to me is that they invoke Bourdieu's (1984) pivotal work, *Distinction*, as part of their explanatory regime, without incorporating any reference to the impacts of class! The irony of this is that *Distinction* is all about class and its role in structuring tastes and preferences.)

10. This is a reference to the book authored by Naomi Klein in 2000, entitled *No Logo*, which became a popular cultural reference within activist cultures in the early twenty-first century.

5 Becoming Actors: Agency and Youth Activist Subcultures

1. It is important to distinguish between the concept of "relationality" as I am using it here, which I situate within a lineage of feminist theorizing about agency, and other ways in which the term "relational" has been used in feminist theory. In this case, I am using the term to indicate the centrality of interpersonal relationships (e.g., friendships, romantic involvements), rather than using it to indicate an opposition (e.g., the ways in which masculinity and femininity are constructed in relation to each other; see, e.g., Rodríguez et al. 2006).
2. In discussing Bourdieu's conception of the relationship between structure and agency, Loïc Wacquant (2005c) notes that "*agency itself is socially structured:* the acts of classification that guide the choices of individuals are systematically oriented by the mental and corporeal schemata resulting from the internalization of the objective patterns of their extant social environment" (137; italics in the original).

Appendix: Research Methods

1. Many of the participants in this project identified as gay, lesbian, bisexual, transgendered, or queer. I thus often encountered them in queer spaces, where I happened to be socially with friends or with my girlfriend. Such queer spaces were often also activist in nature, as there continues to be a great deal of crossover between activist work and queer organizing, particularly in lesbian and trans communities.

2. While I had originally thought to do some comparative work between the different activist cultures across the three cities in which the research took place, I ultimately found far more similarities than differences between my study sites, in both the unspoken rules of activist subcultures as well as participants' experiences of schooling and citizenship education. This may reflect the mobility of middle-class young people across Canada; many of the participants I spoke to in one city had spent time in one of the other study cities, or had grown up in another community in Canada. This is due, in part, to the "hub" nature of Canada's large cities, which tends to draw many young people away from rural or smaller urban communities because of greater opportunities and the appeal of cultural and ethnic diversity. While I do not engage in a sustained comparative analysis of the differences between activist cultures across the three cities, one notable distinction was the explicit anarchist analysis that was prevalent in Montreal, far more developed than in either Toronto or Vancouver. Indeed, those participants who identified with an anarchist analysis in Toronto or Vancouver had inevitably spent time in Montreal. The strength of anarchism as a mode of analysis there may be due to the strong history in Quebec of both separatist activism and trade unionism, a history that seems to have sustained a much more vibrant activist culture across all ages and social locations.
3. Some participants did describe their class identity, generally as either middle class or working class, through the course of our interview. In all cases, their own identification was similar to the one that I subsequently made based on parental occupation.

References

Abu-Laban, Y. "Keeping 'em out: gender, race, and class biases in Canadian immigration policy." In *Painting the maple: essays on race, gender, and the construction of Canada*, edited by V. Strong-Boag, S. Grace, and A. Eisenberg, 69–84. Vancouver: UBC Press, 1998.
Adams, M. L. *The trouble with normal: postwar youth and the making of heterosexuality.* Toronto: University of Toronto Press, 1997.
Adkins, L. "Reflexivity: freedom or habit of gender?" In *Feminism after Bourdieu*, edited by L. Adkins and B. Skeggs, 191–210. Oxford: Blackwell Publishing, 2004.
Agamben, G. *Homo sacer: sovereign power and bare life.* Translated by D. Heller-Roazen. Stanford, California: Stanford University Press, 1998.
Aminzade, R. R., J. A. Goldstone, D. McAdam, E. J. Perry, and W. H. Sewell. *Silence and voice in the study of contentious politics.* New York; Cambridge: Cambridge University Press, 2001.
Anderson, B. *Imagined communities: reflections on the origin and spread of nationalisms.* London & New York: Verso, 2006.
Anderson, S., and J. Cavanaugh. *Field guide to the global economy.* New York: The New Press, 2000.
Anonymous. "Reinventing the Left in Quebec." *Canadian Dimension* 36, no. 4 (2002): 23–26.
Arendt, H. *Between past and future.* New York: Penguin Books, 1968/1993.
———. *The origins of totalitarianism.* Orlando, Florida: Harcourt, Inc., 1968/1994.
———. *The life of the mind.* New York: Harcourt Brace & Company, 1971.
———. *The human condition.* 2nd ed. Chicago: University of Chicago Press, 1998.
Arnot, M., and J. Dillabough. "Feminist politics and democratic values in education." *Curriculum Inquiry* 29, no. 2 (1999): 159–189.

Axelrod, P. *The promise of schooling: education in Canada, 1800–1914.* Toronto: University of Toronto Press, 1997.

Ball, S. J., M. Maguire, and S. Macrae. *Choice, pathways, and transitions post-16: new youth, new economies in the global city.* London; New York: RoutledgeFalmer, 2000.

Bashevkin, S. "Rethinking retrenchment: North American social policy during the early Clinton and Chrétien years." *Canadian Journal of Political Science* 33, no. 1 (2000): 7–36.

Battiste, M., and H. Semaganis. "First thoughts on First Nations citizenship: issues in education." In *Citizenship in Transformation in Canada*, edited by Y. Hebert, 93–111. Toronto: University of Toronto Press, 2002.

Bauman, Z. *Wasted lives: modernity and its outcasts.* Cambridge: Polity Press, 2004.

Beauvais, C., L. McKay, and A. Seddon. *Highlights: youth and the transition to citizenship.* Ottawa: Canadian Policy Research Network, 2001.

Beck, U. *World risk society.* Malden, MA: Blackwell Publishers Inc., 1999.

Bello, W. "The iron cage: the World Trade Organization, the Bretton Woods Institutions, and the South." *Capitalism, Nature, Socialism* 11, no. 1 (2000): 3–32.

Benhabib, S. "Subjectivity, historiography, and politics: reflections on the 'feminism/postmodernism exchange.'" In *Feminist contentions: a philosophical exchange*, edited by S. Benhabib, J. Butler, D. Cornell, and N. Fraser, 107–126. New York and London: Routledge, 1995.

———. "Toward a deliberative model of democratic legitimacy." In *Democracy and difference: contesting the boundaries of the political*, edited by S. Benhabib, 67–94. Princeton, NJ: Princeton University Press, 1996.

———. "Sexual difference and collective identities: the new global constellation." *Signs: Journal of Women in Culture and Society* 24, no. 2 (1999): 335–361.

———. *The rights of others: aliens, residents and citizens.* Cambridge; New York: Cambridge University Press, 2004.

Benhabib, S., J. Butler, D. Cornell, and N. Fraser. *Feminist contentions: a philosophical exchange.* New York: Routledge, 1995.

Bennett, A. "Researching youth culture and popular music: a methodological critique." *British Journal of Sociology* 53, no. 3 (2002): 451–466.

Bennett, A., and K. Kahn-Harris. "Introduction." In *After subculture: critical studies in contemporary youth culture*, edited by A. Bennett and K. Kahn-Harris, 1–18. New York: Palgrave-MacMillan, 2004.
Best, R. "New bottles for old wine? Affective education and the 'citizenship revolution' in English schools." *Pastoral Care in Education* 21, no. 4 (2003): 14–21.
Bettie, J. *Women without class: girls, race, and identity*. Berkeley: University of California Press, 2003.
Bondi, L. "Working the spaces of neoliberal subjectivity: psychotherapeutic technologies, professionalisation and counselling." *Antipode* 37, no. 3 (2005): 497–514.
Bourdieu, P. *Distinction: a social critique of the judgement of taste*. Translated by R. Nice. Cambridge, Massachusetts: Harvard University Press, 1984.
———. *Language and symbolic power*. Translated by G. Raymond and M. Adamson. Cambridge, Massachusetts: Harvard University Press, 1991.
———. *Pascalian meditations*. Translated by R. Nice. Stanford, California: Stanford University Press, 1997.
———. *The weight of the world: social suffering in contemporary society*. Translated by P. P. Ferguson. Stanford, California: Stanford University Press, 1999.
———. "The mystery of ministry: from particular wills to the general will." In *Pierre Bourdieu and democratic politics*, edited by L. Wacquant, 55–63. Cambridge, UK: Polity Press, 2005.
———. *Outline of a theory of practice*. Cambridge: Cambridge University Press, 2006/1977.
Bourdieu, P., and L. Wacquant. *An invitation to reflexive sociology*. Chicago & London: University of Chicago Press, 1992.
Brand, D. *Bread out of stone: recollections, sex, recognition, race, dreaming, politics*. Toronto: Coach House Press, 1994.
British Columbia Ministry of Education. "Civic studies 11: integrated resource package 2005." (2005). http://www.bced.gov.bc.ca/irp/civic11.pdf (March 23, 2007).
———. "Graduation Transitions." (2007). http://www.bced.gov.bc.ca/graduation/grad-transitions/welcome.htm (November 22, 2007).
Britzman, D. P. "Beyond innocent readings: educational ethnography as a crisis of representation." In *Continuity and contradiction: the futures of the sociology of education*, edited by W. T. Pink and G. W. Noblit, 133–156. Cresskill, NJ: Hampton Press, 1995.

Brodie, J. "Three stories of Canadian citizenship." In *Contesting Canadian citizenship: historical readings*, edited by R. Adamoski, D. E. Chunn, and R. Menzies, 43–68. Peterborough: Broadview Press, 2002.

Brown, W. *States of injury: power and freedom in late modernity*. Princeton, NJ: Princeton University Press, 1995.

———. *Politics out of history*. Princeton, NJ: Princeton University Press, 2001.

———. *Edgework: critical essays on knowledge and politics*. Princeton and Oxford: Princeton University Press, 2005.

———. *Regulating aversion: tolerance in the age of identity and empire*. Princeton and Oxford: Princeton University Press, 2006.

Butler, J. "Contingent foundations: feminism and the question of 'postmodernism.'" In *Feminist contentions: A philosophical exchange*, edited by S. Benhabib, J. Butler, D. Cornell, and N. Fraser, 35–58. New York and London: Routledge, 1995a.

———. "For a careful reading." In *Feminist contentions: A philosophical exchange*, edited by S. Benhabib, J. Butler, D. Cornell, and N. Fraser, 127–144. London: Routledge, 1995b.

Bynner, J. "The challenge of citizenship for youth study." In *Youth, citizenship and social change in a European context*, edited by J. Bynner, L. Chisholm, and A. Furlong, 234–241. Brookfield, USA: Ashgate, 1997.

Bynner, J., L. Chisholm, and A. Furlong. "A new agenda for youth research." In *Youth, citizenship and social change in a European context*, edited by J. Bynner, L. Chisholm, and A. Furlong, 3-14. Brookfield, USA: Ashgate, 1997.

Cambre, C. "Revolution within the revolution: a Caracas collective and the face of Che Guevara." *Review of Education, Pedagogy, and Cultural Studies* 31, no. 4 (2009): 338–364.

Campaign 2000. "2007 report card on child and family poverty in Canada." (2007). http://www.campaign2000.ca/rc/rc07/2007_C2000_NationalReportCard.pdf (January 14, 2008).

Canadian Labour Congress. "Canada among countries cited for growing anti-union repression." Press release, June 10, 2003. http://canadianlabour.ca/index.php/june_28/168 (August 8, 2006).

Carroll, B., and R. Jones. "The road to innovation, conversion or inertia: Devolution in housing policy in Canada." *Canadian Public Policy* 26, no. 3 (2000): 277–294.

Carroll, W. K. *Organizing dissent: contemporary social movements in theory and practice.* Toronto: Garamond Press, 1992.
Chamberlin, R. "Citizenship? Only if you haven't got a life: secondary school pupils' views of citizenship education." *Westminster Studies in Education* 26, no. 2 (2003): 87–97.
Chomsky, N. *Profit over people: neoliberalism and global order.* New York: Seven Stories Press, 1999.
Clarke, J., S. Hall, T. Jefferson, and B. Roberts. "Subcultures, cultures and class." In *Resistance through rituals: youth subcultures in post-war Britain*, edited by S. Hall and T. Jefferson, 9–79. New York: Routledge, 1976.
Coates, K. "Being Aboriginal: the cultural politics of identity, membership, and belonging among First Nations in Canada." In *Aboriginal Peoples in Canada: Futures and Identities*, edited by M. Behiels, 23–41. Montreal: Association for Canadian Studies, 1999.
Cohen, P. *Rethinking the youth question: education, labour and cultural studies.* Houndmills, Basingstoke, Hampshire: Macmillan, 1997.
Cohen, S. *Folk devils and moral panics.* 3rd ed. Routledge: London & New York, 1972/2002.
Conway, J. *Identity, place, knowledge: social movements contesting globalization.* Halifax: Fernwood Publishing, 2004.
Coole, D. *Women in political theory: from ancient misogyny to contemporary feminism.* Herfordshire: Harvester Wheatsheaf, 1993.
Cornell, D. "What is ethical feminism?." In *Feminist contentions: a philosophical exchange*, edited by S. Benhabib, J. Butler, D. Cornell, and N. Fraser, 75–106. New York and London: Routledge, 1995.
Council of Canadians. "Council of Canadians shocked that the WTO set to negotiate away our water." Media release, 2001. http://www.canadians.org/browse_categories.htm?COC_token=23@@a6e1eefb289769c3f2dd41e2fc231081&step=2&catid=187&iscat=1 (August 8, 2006).
Criddle, E., M. O'Neill, and L. Vidovich. "Discovering democracy: an analysis of curriculum policy for citizenship education." *Westminster Studies in Education* 27, no. 1 (2004): 27–41.
Crossley, N. "The phenomenological habitus and its construction." *Theory and Society* 30, no. 1 (2001): 81–120.
Curtis, B. "State of the nation or community of spirit? Schooling for civic and ethnic-religious nationalism in insurrectionary Canada." *History of Education Quarterly* 43, no. 3 (2003): 325–349.
Curtis, K. *Our sense of the real: aesthetic experience and Arendtian politics.* Ithaca and London: Cornell University Press, 1999.

Davies, I., S. Gorard, and N. McGuinn. "Citizenship education and character education: similarities and constraints." *British Journal of Educational Studies* 53, no. 3 (2005): 341–358.

Day, R. J. F. *Gramsci is dead: anarchist undercurrents in the newest social movements*. Toronto: Between The Lines, 2005.

de Broucker, P. *Without a paddle: what to do about Canada's young drop-outs*. Ottawa: Canadian Policy Research Network, 2005.

Dean, A. *Locking them up to keep them "safe": criminalized girls in British Columbia*. Vancouver, BC: Justice for Girls, 2005.

DePass, C., and S. Qureshi. "Paradoxes, contradictions, and ironies of democratic citizenship education." In *Citizenship in transformation in Canada*, edited by Y. Hebert, 175–190. Toronto: University of Toronto Press, 2002.

DiMascio, A. "Educational discourse and the making of educational legislation in early Upper Canada." *History of Education Quarterly* 50, no. 1 (2010): 34–54.

Dillabough, J. "Class, culture and the 'predicaments of masculine domination': Encountering Pierre Bourdieu." *British Journal of Sociology of Education* 25, no. 4 (2004): 489–506.

Dillabough, J., and J. Kennelly. *Lost youth in the global city: class, culture, and the urban imaginary*. New York: Routledge, 2010.

Dillabough, J., E. Wang, and J. Kennelly. "'Ginas,' 'thugs,' and 'gangstas': young people's struggles to 'become somebody' in working-class urban Canada." *Journal of Curriculum Theorizing* 21, no. 2 (2005): 83–108.

Dillabough, J., J. Kennelly. and E. Wang. "Spatial containment in the inner city: youth subcultures, class conflict and geographies of exclusion." In *The way class works: readings on school, family, and the economy*, edited by L. Weis, 329–346. New York and London: Routledge, 2008.

Dobbin, M. "Liberal or neoliberal?." (2003). http://www.policy-alternatives.ca/index.cfm?act=news&call=840&do=article&pA=B B736455 (August 8, 2006).

Edwards, F., and D. Mercer. "Gleaning from gluttony: an Australian youth subculture confronts the ethics of waste." *Australian Geographer* 38, no. 3 (2007): 279–296.

Fanelli, C., and J. Paulson. "Municipal malaise: neoliberal urbanism and the future of our cities." *Relay: A Socialist Project Review* 29 (2010): 4–9.

Fine, M., L. Weis, S. Weseen, and L. Wong. "For whom? Qualitative research, representations, and social responsibilities." In *The landscape of qualitative research*, edited by N. K. Denzin and Y. S. Lincoln, 167–207. Thousand Oaks, California: Sage, 2003.

Foucault, M. "Governmentality." In *The Foucault effect: Studies in governmentality*, edited by G. Burchell, C. Gordon, and P. Miller, 53–72. Chicago: University of Chicago Press, 1991.

———. "The political technology of individuals." Vol. 3. In *Power: Essential works of Foucault 1954–1984*, edited by J. D. Faubian, 403–417. New York: The New Press, 1994a.

———. "The subject and power." Vol. 3. In *Power: Essential works of Foucault 1954–1984*, edited by J. D. Faubian, 326–348. New York: The New Press, 1994b.

France, A. "Why should we care?: Young people, citizenship and questions of social responsibility." *Journal of Youth Studies* 1, no. 1 (1998): 97–111.

Fraser, N., and L. Gordon. "A genealogy of dependency: tracing a keyword of the U.S. welfare state." *Signs: Journal of Women in Culture and Society* 19, no. 2 (1994): 309–336.

Frazer, E., and N. Emler. "Participation and citizenship: a new agenda for youth politics research?" In *Youth, citizenship and social change in a European context*, edited by J. Bynner, L. Chisholm, and A. Furlong, 171–195. Brookfield, USA: Ashgate, 1997.

Frideres, J. S. "Education for Indians vs Indian education in Canada." *The Indian Historian* 11, no. 1 (1978): 29–35.

Fuller, S. "Editorial: Was your tax cut worth it?" (2001). http://www.policyalternatives.ca/index.cfm?act=news&call=659&do=article&pA=BB736455 (August 10, 2006).

Gallagher, K. *The theatre of urban: youth and schooling in dangerous times*. Toronto: University of Toronto Press, 2007.

Gauvreau, M. "The protracted birth of the Canadian 'teenager': Work, citizenship, and the Canadian Youth Commission, 1943–1955." In *Cultures of citizenship in post-war Canada, 1940–1955*, edited by N. Christie and M. Gauvreau, 201–238. Montreal and Kingston: McGill-Queen's University Press, 2003.

Give Us The Keys. "Remember the Pope Squat? The real campaign is about to begin in Parkdale." (2006). http://www.rabble.ca/babble/ultimatebb.cgi?ubb=get_topic&f=9&t=001518&p= (December 31, 2007).

Gordon, H. *We fight to win: inequality and the politics of youth activism*. New Jersey: Rutgers University Press, 2010.

Gordon, T., J. Holland, and E. Lahelma. "From pupil to citizen: a gendered route." In *Challenging democracy: international perspectives on gender, education, and citizenship*, edited by M. Arnot and J. Dillabough, 187–202. London and New York: Routledge, 2000.

Graeber, D. *Direct action: an ethnography*. Oakland, CA: AK Press, 2009.

Habermas, J. "Three normative models of democracy." In *Democracy and difference: contesting the boundaries of the political*, edited by S. Benhabib, 21–30. Princeton, NJ: Princeton University Press, 1996.

Hall, S. "Signification, representation, ideology: Althusser and the post-structuralist debates." *Critical Studies in Mass Communication* 2, no. 2 (1985): 91–114.

Hall, T., A. Coffey, and H. Williamson. "Self, space and place: youth identities and citizenship." *British Journal of Sociology of Education* 20, no. 4 (1999): 501–513.

Hargrave, C. "Homeless in Canada: from housing to shelters to blankets." (1999). Share International. http://www.shareintl.org/archives/homelessness/hl-ch_Canada.htm (August 8, 2006).

Harper, D. "On the authority of the image: visual methods at the crossroads." In *Collecting and interpreting qualitative materials*, edited by N. K. Denzin and Y. S. Lincoln, 130–149. Thousands Oaks: Sage Publications, 1998.

Harris, A. *Future girl: young women in the twenty-first century*. New York and London: Routledge, 2004.

———. "Introduction." In *Next wave cultures: feminism, subcultures, activism*, edited by A. Harris, 1–13. New York and London: Routledge, 2008.

Heath, J., and A. Potter. *The rebel sell: why the culture can't be jammed*. Toronto: HarperCollins Publishers Ltd, 2004.

Hebdige, D. *Subculture: the meaning of style*. New York: Methuen & Co., Ltd., 1979.

Hébert, Y. "Citizenship education: towards a pedagogy of social participation and identity formation." *Canadian Ethnic Studies* 29, no. 2 (1997): 82–97.

Hernández, A. *Pedagogy, democracy and feminism: rethinking the public sphere*. Albany, NY: State University of New York Press, 1997.

Highlander Research and Education Center. "A tribute to Rosa Parks." (2005). http://www.highlandercenter.org/n-rosa-parks.asp (August 31, 2007).

Ichilov, O. "Pride in one's country and citizenship orientations in a divided society: the case of Israeli-Palestinian Arab and Orthodox and Non-Orthodix Jewish Israeli youth." *Comparative Education Review* 49, no. 1 (2005): 44–61.

Institute for Public Policy Research. "Childhood is changing, but 'paedophobia' makes things worse." (2006). http://www.ippr.org.uk/pressreleases/?id=2388 (November 28, 2007).

Joshee, R. "Citizenship and multicultural education in Canada: from assimilation to social cohesion." In *Diversity and citizenship education: global perspectives*, edited by J. A. Banks, 127–156. San Francisco: Jossey-Bass, 2004.

Keil, R. "'Common sense' neoliberalism: progressive conservative urbanism in Toronto, Canada." *Antipode* 34, no. 3 (2002): 578–601.

Kennelly, J. "Policing young people as citizens-in-waiting: legitimacy, spatiality, and governance." *British Journal of Criminology*, no. 51 (2011): 336–354.

Kennelly, J., and J. Dillabough. "Young people mobilizing the language of citizenship: struggles for classification and new meaning in an uncertain world." *British Journal of Sociology of Education* 29, no. 5 (2008): 493–508.

Kennelly, J., and K. Llewellyn. "Educating for active compliance: discursive constructions in citizenship education." *Citizenship Studies* (in press).

Kershaw, P. "'Choice' discourse in BC child care: distancing policy from research." *Canadian Journal of Political Science* 37, no. 4 (2004): 927–950.

Kirkness, V., and S. Bowman. *First Nations schools: triumphs and struggles*. Toronto: Canadian Education Association, 1992.

Klein, N. *No logo: taking aim at the brand bullies*. New York: Knopf Canada, 2000.

Langdridge, D. "The hermeneutic phenomenology of Paul Ricoeur." *Existential Analysis* 15, no. 2 (2004): 243–255.

Lather, P. "Postmodernism, post-structuralism and post(critical) ethnography: of ruins, aporias and angels." In *Handbook of ethnography*, edited by P. Atkinson et al., 477–492. Thousand Oaks: Sage Publications, 2001.

Lawler, S. "Rules of engagement: habitus, power, and resistance." In *Feminism after Bourdieu*, edited by L. Adkins and B. Skeggs, 110–128. Oxford: Blackwell Publishing, 2004.

Leighton, R. "The nature of citizenship education provision: an initial study." *The Curriculum Journal* 15, no. 2 (2004): 167–181.

Létourneau, J. "Remembering our past: an examination of the historical memory of young Québecois." In *To the past: history education, public memory, and citizenship in Canada*, edited by R. W. Sandwell, 70–87. Toronto: University of Toronto Press, 2006.

Levinson, B. "Hopes and challenges for the new civic education in Mexico: toward a democratic citizen without adjectives." *International Journal of Educational Development* 24 (2003): 269–282.

Levitt, C. *Children of privilege: student revolt in the sixties.* Toronto: University of Toronto Press, 1984.

Lister, R. *Citizenship: feminist perspectives.* New York: New York University Press, 2003.

London Feminist Salon Collective. "The problematization of agency in postmodern theory: as feminist educational researchers, where do we go from here?" *Gender and Education* 16, no. 1 (2004): 25–33.

Lousely, C. "(De)politicizing the environment club: environmental discourses and the culture of schooling." *Environmental Education Research* 5, no. 3 (1999): 293–305.

Lovell, T. "Thinking feminism with and against Bourdieu." *Feminist Theory* 1, no. 1 (2000): 11–32.

———. "Resisting with authority: historical specificity, agency and the performative self." *Theory, Culture and Society* 20, no. 1 (2003): 1–17.

Low, B. J. "'The new generation': mental hygiene and the portrayals of children by the National Film Board of Canada, 1946–1967." *History of Education Quarterly* 43, no. 4 (2003): 540–570.

Lucey, H., and D. Reay. "A market in waste: psychic and structural dimensions of school-choice policy in the UK and children's narratives on 'demonized' schools." *Discourse: studies in the cultural politics of education* 23, no. 3 (2002): 253–266.

Luttrell, W. "Becoming somebody in and against school: toward a psychocultural theory of gender and self-making." In *The cultural production of the educated person: critical ethnographies of schooling and local practice*, edited by B. A. Levinson, D. E. Foley, and D. C. Holland, 93–117. Albany, NY: State University of New York, 1996.

Marcuse, H. *One-dimensional man: studies in the ideology of advanced industrial society.* Boston: Beacon Press, 1991/1964.

Marshall, T. H. "Citizenship and social class." In *Citizenship and social class*, edited by T. H. Marshall and T. Bottomore, 3–51. London: Pluto Press, 1992/1950.

Martin, P. J. "Culture, subculture, and social organization." In *After subculture: critical studies in contemporary youth culture*, edited by A. Bennett and K. Kahn-Harris. New York: Palgrave-MacMillan, 2004.

Mata, F. "Visible minorities as citizens and workers in Canada." In *Citizenship in transformation in Canada*, edited by Y. Hébert, 191–208. Toronto: University of Toronto Press, 2002.

Mazurek, K., and N. Kach. "Multiculturalism, society and education." In *Canadian education: historical themes and contemporary issues*, edited by B. Titley, 133–160. Calgary: Detselig Enterprises Ltd, 1990.

McDonald, K. *Global movements: action and culture*. Malden, MA: Blackwell Publishing, 2006.

McLeod, J. "Feminists re-reading Bourdieu: old debates and new questions about gender habitus and gender change." *Theory and Research in Education* 3, no. 1 (2005): 11–30.

McLeod, J., and L. Yates. *Making modern lives: subjectivity, schooling, and social change*. New York: State University of New York Press, 2006.

McNay, L. "Gender and narrative identity." *Journal of Political Ideologies* 4, no. 3 (1999a): 215–336.

———. "Subject, psyche and agency: the work of Judith Butler." *Theory, Culture and Society* 16, no. 2 (1999b): 175–193.

———. *Gender and agency: reconfiguring the subject in feminist and social theory*. Cambridge: Polity Press, 2000.

———. "Agency, anticipation and indeterminacy in feminist theory." *Feminist Theory* 4, no. 2 (2003a): 139–148.

———. "Having it both ways: The incompatibility of narrative identity and communicative ethics in feminist thought." *Theory, Culture and Society* 20, no. 6 (2003b): 1–20.

———. "Agency and experience: gender as a lived relation." In *Feminism after Bourdieu*, edited by L. Adkins and B. Skeggs, 175–190. Oxford: Blackwell Publishing, 2004.

McRobbie, A. *Feminism and youth culture: from Jackie to Just Seventeen*. Boston: Unwin Hyman, Inc, 1991.

———. *Postmodernism and popular culture*. New York: Routledge, 1994.

Media Release. "McGuinty government supports character development in schools: new initiative will help students achieve potential, become involved citizens. (2006)." http://www.premier.gov.on.ca/news/Product.asp?ProductID=802 (March 18, 2007).

Melucci, A. *Nomads of the present: social movements and individual needs in contemporary society*. Philadelphia: Temple University Press, 1989.

Mitchell, K. "Educating the national citizen in neoliberal times: from the multicultural self to the strategic cosmopolitan." *Transactions of the Institute of British Geographers* 28 (2003): 387–403.

Mizen, P. "Putting the politics back into youth studies: Keynesianism, monetarism and the changing state of youth." *Journal of Youth Studies* 5, no. 1 (2002): 5–20.

Moore, R. "Cultural capital: objective probability and the cultural arbitrary." *British Journal of Sociology of Education* 25, no. 4 (2004): 445–456.

Mouffe, C. *The return of the political.* London; New York: Verso, 1993.

Numerous authors. "An open letter on movement building." (2003). http://www.zmag.org/content/showarticle.cfm?SectionID =30&ItemID=3100 (February 27, 2007).

Ong, A. "Cultural citizenship as subject-making: immigrants negotiate racial and cultural boundaries in the United States." *Current Anthropology* 37, no. 5 (1996): 737–762.

Ontario Ministry of Training, Colleges and Universities. "Choosing high school diploma requirements (2006)." http://www.edu.gov. on.ca/eng/document/brochure/stepup/high.html (November 22, 2007).

Ortner, S. *New Jersey dreaming: capital, culture, and the class of '58.* Durham and London: Duke University Press, 2003.

Osborne, K. "Public schooling and citizenship education in Canada." *Canadian Ethnic Studies* 32, no. 1 (2000): 8–38.

Osler, A., and H. Starkey. "Learning for cosmopolitan citizenship: theoretical debates and young people's experiences." *Educational Review* 55, no. 3 (2003): 243–254.

Palmer, B. D. *Canada's 1960s: the ironies of identity in a rebellious era.* Toronto: University of Toronto Press, 2009.

Pammett, J. H., and L. LeDuc. "Confronting the problem of declining voter turnout among youth." *Electoral Insight* 5, no. 2 (2003): 3–9.

Persson, D. "The changing experience of Indian residential schooling: Blue Quills, 1931–1970." In *Indian Education in Canada, Volume 2: The Challenge,* edited by J. Barman, Y. Hebert, and D. McCaskill, 150–168. Vancouver: UBC Press, 1986.

Phillips, A. *Democracy and difference.* Cambridge: Polity Press, 1993.

Prentice, A. *The school promoters: Education and social class in mid-nineteenth century Upper Canada.* Oxford; New York: Oxford University Press, 1999.

Public Health Agency of Canada. "Backgrounder: improving the health and wellbeing of Canada's youth." (2002). http://www. phac-aspc.gc.ca/ph-sp/phdd/report/toward/back/well.html (August 8, 2006).

Raco, M. "Governmentality, subject-building, and the discourses and practices of devolution in the UK." *Transactions of the Institute of British Geographers* 28 (2003): 75–95.

Reay, D. " 'It's all becoming a habitus': beyond the habitual use of habitus in educational research." *British Journal of Sociology of Education* 25, no. 4 (2004): 431–444.

Ricoeur, P. *Hermeneutics and the human sciences*. Translated by J. B. Thompson. Cambridge, UK: Cambridge University Press, 1998/1981.

Robert, D. "Are we losing Quebec to neoliberals?" *Canadian Dimension* 31, no. 2 (1997): 15–18.

Rodríguez, M., J. V. Piña, C. M. Fernández, and M. P. Viñuela. "Gender discourse about an ethic of care: nursery schoolteachers' perspectives." *Gender and Education* 18, no. 2 (2006): 183–197.

Rose, N. "Governing the enterprising self." In *The values of the enterprise culture: the moral debate*, edited by P. Heelas and P. Morris, 141–164. London and New York: Routledge, 1992.

———. "Government, authority, and expertise in advanced liberalism." *Economy and Society* 22, no. 3 (1993): 283–299.

———. *Inventing ourselves: psychology, power, and personhood*. Cambridge and New York: Cambridge University Press, 1998.

———. *Powers of freedom: reframing political thought*. New York: Cambridge University Press, 1999.

Rose, N., P. O'Malley, and M. Valverde. "Governmentality." *Annual Review of Law and Society* 2 (2006): 83–104.

Ross, B. "A lesbian politics of erotic decolonization." In *Painting the Maple: essays on race, gender, and the construction of Canada*, edited by V. Strong-Boag, S. Grace, and A. Eisenberg, 187–214. Vancouver: UBC Press, 1998.

Sangster, J. "Creating social and moral citizens: defining and treating delinquent boys and girls in English Canada, 1920–65." In *Contesting Canadian citizenship: historical readings*, edited by R. Adamoski, D. E. Chunn, and R. Menzies, 337–358. Peterborough: Broadview Press, 2002.

Scott-Bauman, A. "Citizenship and postmodernity." *Intercultural education* 14, no. 4 (2003): 355–366.

Sewell Jr., W. H. "A theory of structure: duality, agency and transformation." *American Journal of Sociology* 98, no. 1 (1992): 1–29.

Siltanen, J. "Paradise paved? Reflections on the fate of social citizenship in Canada." *Citizenship Studies* 6, no. 4 (2002): 395–414.

Skeggs, B. *Class, self, culture*. London and New York: Routledge, 2004.

Smith, L. T. *Decolonizing methodologies. Research and Indigenous peoples.* New York: Zed Books Ltd, 1999.

Sparks, H. "Dissident citizenship: democratic theory, political courage, and activist women." *Hypatia* 12, no. 4 (1997): 74–104.

Stanley, T. J. "Bringing anti-racism into historical explanation: the Victoria Chinese Students' strike of 1922–3 revisited." *Journal of the Canadian Historical Association* 13 (2002): 141–165.

———. "Whose public? Whose memory? Racisms, grand narratives, and Canadian history." In *To the past: history education, public memory, and citizenship in Canada*, edited by R. W. Sandwell, 32–49. Toronto: University of Toronto Press, 2006.

Starr, A. *Naming the enemy: anti-corporate movements confront globalization.* London and New York: Zed Books Ltd, 2001.

Stasiulis, D. "The active child citizen: lessons from Canadian policy and the children's movement." *Citizenship Studies* 6, no. 4 (2002): 507–538.

Statistics Canada,. "National graduates survey: student debt." (2004). *The Daily.* http://www.statcan.ca/Daily/English/040426 /d040426a.htm (August 6, 2006).

Stryker, S., T. J. Owens, and R. W. White. *Self, identity and social movements.* Vol. 13. Minneapolis, London: University of Minnesota Press, 2000.

Taylor, L. "A public lesson in fear and apathy: educators condemn the G20 attack on civic education." (2010). http://www.petitononline.com/Educator/petition.html (October 4, 2010).

Thornton, S. *Club cultures: music, media, and subcultural capital.* Middletown, CT: Wesleyan University Press, 1996.

Tilley, C. *From mobilization to revolution.* Reading, Mass.: Addision-Wesley, 1978.

———. "Models and realities of popular collective action." *Social Research* 52, no. 4 (1985): 745–750.

Tilley, C., and S. Tarrow. *Contentious politics.* Boulder, Colorado: Paradigm Publishers, 2007.

Titley, B. "Editor's introduction." In *Canadian education: historical themes and contemporary issues,* edited by B. Titley, 81–82. Calgary: Detselig Enterprises Ltd., 1990.

Titley, B., and K. Mazurek. "Back to the basics? Forward to the fundamentals?" In *Canadian education: historical themes and contemporary issues,* edited by B. Titley, 111–125. Calgary: Detselig Enterprises Ltd., 1990.

Touraine, A. *The voice and the eye: an analysis of social movements.* Translated by A. Duff. Cambridge: Cambridge University Press, 1981.

———. *Return of the actor: social theory in postindustrial society.* Translated by M. Godzich. Minneapolis: University of Minnesota Press, 1988.
Turner, D. "Horizons revealed: from methodology to method." *International Journal of Qualitative Methods* 2, no. 1 (2003): 1–32.
Wacquant, L. "Critical thought as solvent of doxa." *Constellations* 11, no. 1 (2004): 97–101.
———. "Introduction: symbolic power and democratic practice." In *Pierre Bourdieu and democratic politics*, edited by L. Wacquant, 1–9. Cambridge, UK: Polity Press, 2005a.
———. "Pointers on Pierre Bourdieu and democratic politics." In *Pierre Bourdieu and democratic politics*, edited by L. Wacquant, 10–28. Cambridge, UK: Polity Press, 2005b.
———. "Symbolic power in the rule of the 'state nobility.'" In *Pierre Bourdieu and democratic politics*, edited by L. Wacquant, 133–150. Cambridge, UK: Polity Press, 2005c.
Walkerdine, V., and H. Lucey. *Democracy in the kitchen: regulating mothers and socialising daughters.* London: Virago, 1989.
Walkerdine, V., H. Lucey, and J. Melody. *Growing up girl: psychosocial explorations in gender and class.* Houndmills: Palgrave-MacMillan, 2001.
Walsh, P. "Education and the 'universalist' idiom of empire: Irish National School Books in Ireland and Ontario." *History of Education* 37, no. 5 (2008): 645–660.
Weller, S. *Teenagers' citizenship: experiences and education.* New York and London: Routledge, 2007.
Westheimer, J., and Kahne, J., "What kind of citizen? The politics of educating for democracy." Paper presented at the Canadian Society for the Study of Education, Halifax, Nova Scotia, 2003.
Williams, R. *Marxism and Literature.* Oxford: Oxford University Press, 1977.
———. *Resources of hope: culture, democracy, socialism.* New York: Verso, 1989.
Willis, P. *Learning to labour: how working class kids get working class jobs.* New York: Columbia University Press, 1977.
———. *Common culture: symbolic work at play in the everyday cultures of the young.* Buckingham: Open University Press, 1990.
———. *The ethnographic imagination.* Cambridge: Polity Press, 2000.
Yates, M., and J. Younnis. *Roots of civic identity: international perspectives on community service and activism in youth.* Cambridge, UK: Cambridge University Press, 1999.

Young, I. M. *Justice and the politics of difference.* Princeton, NJ: Princeton University Press, 1990.

Young, J. *The exclusive society: social exclusion, crime and difference in late modernity.* London: Sage, 1999.

Young, J. R. "Equality of opportunity: reality or myth?" In *Canadian education: historical themes and contemporary issues*, edited by B. Titley, 161–171. Calgary: Detselig Enterprises Ltd., 1990.

Young-Bruehl, E. *Hannah Arendt: for love of the world.* New Haven and London: Yale University Press, 1982.

———. *Why Arendt matters.* New Haven and London: Yale University Press, 2006.

Zald, M., and J. D. McCarthy, eds. *The dynamics of social movements.* Cambridge, Mass.: Winthrop Publishers Inc., 1979.

Zizek, S. "Against human rights." *New Left Review* 34 (2005): 115–131.

Index

Aboriginal peoples, 37–39, 84
Abu-Laban, Y., 42, 69, 157
"active citizens," 70, 91–92, 102, 131, 162–163n4
activism, cultural field of, 15–16, 58–59, 74–78, 88, 99, 121, 128
See also youth activism
activist communities, 64
activist habitus
   acquiring and being "invited in," 117–123, 136–137
   agency and, 112–113, 116–117
   developing, 78–82
   habitus shift, 116
   notion of, 75–78
   race and, 34, 71, 82–90
   relationships and exclusion, 125–129, 130
   relationships and inclusion, 123–125, 130
activist icons, 81
Adams, M. L., 40
Adkins, L., 122
adolescence, notion of, 26
adulthood, notion of, 25–26
Agamben, G., 164n6
agency
   activist subcultures and, 111–112
   feminist debates and, 112–117
   habitus and, 112–113, 116–117
   relational agency, 17, 109, 112, 125–129, 131, 136, 139, 166n1
aggressive policing, 66–70
Aminzade, R. R., 11

Anderson, B., 87
Anderson, S., 6
An invitation to reflexive sociology (Wacquant), 138, 145, 165n8
anticolonialism, 4, 11, 134, 144
anticonsumerism, 96
antiglobalization, 11, 134, 155
antipoverty movements, 11, 50–53, 120, 163n2
antiwar movements, 11
Arendt, H., 29–30, 58, 69, 71, 87, 111, 126, 141, 164
Are You Popular? (film), 40
Arnot, M., 60
Australia, 37
authority, discipline and, 99–107
authorized language, 13, 16, 99–101, 115, 121, 129
autonomy, youth, 25–29
Axelrod, P., 35–37

"bad activist" *vs.* "good citizen," 3, 16, 50–52, 65, 123
Ball, S. J., 5
Bashevkin, S., 6
Battiste, M., 37
Bauman, Z., 5
Beauvais, C., 6
Beck, U., 5
Bello, W., 6
"belonging," feeling of, 86–89, 97–98, 104–105, 117–123, 136
Benhabib, S., 29, 69, 87, 112–113, 140
Bennett, A., 13, 146

Best, R., 10, 44
Bettie, J., 74, 77, 83, 96, 136, 147, 153
Birmingham Centre for Contemporary Cultural Studies, 12
boat-naming, 100
Bondi, L., 23
Bouchard, L., 7
Bourdieu, P., 11–12, 15–16, 45, 49, 56, 73, 74–79, 93–94, 99, 103, 109, 112–115, 125, 129, 137–138, 145, 165n8, 165n9, 166n2
Bowman, S., 38
Brand, D., 164
British Columbia
  citizenship curriculum in, 44, 54
  conservative politics in, 7–8
  Ministry of Education, 50, 52, 162
British values, influence of, 7, 35–38
Britzman, D. P., 144
Brodie, J., 41–42
Brown, W., 5–6, 17, 20, 23–25, 53, 56, 66, 71
Butler, J., 112–113
Bynner, J., 5, 26–27, 162, 162n2

Cambre, C., 81
Campaign 2000, 161
Campbell, G., 7
Canadian Labour Congress, 6
"can-do" girls, 60
capitalist state, 27–29, 45, 47
Carroll, B., 6, 9
Carroll, W. K., 10
Cavanaugh, J., 6
Chamberlin, R., 9
"change the world" ideals, 58, 60, 64
Charest, J., 7
Che, 81
childhood, notion of, 25–26, 80
Chisholm, L., 5

Chomsky, N., 6, 89, 108
citizenship, concept of
  "common sense" notions of citizenship, 39, 47–48, 82, 125, 128
  "informed citizenship," 44–45
  non-normative concepts, 43–45
  overview, 9–14, 21, 41–44, 70, 140
  power relations and, 19, 20, 21, 25–26, 134
  "responsibility" and, 45, 65–66, 70–71, 140, 162–163n
  youth inclusion in, 30, 162n2, 165n8
  See also "good citizen," notion of; youth citizenship
citizenship education
  activist engagement and, 53–55, 70
  British values, influence of, 7, 35–38
  for civil order, 35–36
  class divisions and, 39–40, 90–99
  curriculum examples, 50–51, 52–55
  funding for, 42–43
  gender and, 38–39
  history of, 162nn1–2
  multiculturalism in, 43
  neoliberalism and, 25–26
  pessimism about young people in, 8–14, 33, 45, 54–55, 140
  progressive education, 41–44
  public schooling and, 35–36, 162n1
  race and, 34, 37–39, 41
  for respectability/moral norms, 39–40
  role of schooling in, 33–35
  social welfare and, 41–43
  societal views about, 39–45
  standardized exams, 42, 43
civil rights movements, 115–116
Clarke, J., 12

Index

class divisions/class exclusion, 73
  activist engagement and, 78–82, 135
  activist habitus and, 129–130
  activists, perceptions of and, 64–65
  in activist subcultures, 90–99, 107–109, 119
  citizenship education and, 39–40, 90–99, 165n9
  family history and, 78–82, 117–118
  "middle-class performance," 77–83, 94–98, 109, 134–136, 140
  race and, 82–84
  symbolic economy, subcultural, 74–78
  "working-class performance," 77, 83, 94–98, 109, 134, 136
class histories, 155–156
classification, forms of, 11, 35–39, 45, 166n1
"class performance," 77, 83, 94–98, 109, 134, 136
Coates, K., 38
Coffey, A., 10
"cognitive structures," 75
Cohen, P., 12, 76
Cohen, S., 9
colonialism
  anticolonialism, 4, 11, 134, 144
  history of, 6, 82, 109, 117, 130, 133
colonialist expansion, 4, 35–37
"common sense" notions of citizenship, 39, 47–48, 82, 125, 128
community participation *vs.* individualism, 57–59
community work, 52–53
conservative political views, 7–8
  See also neoliberalism
consumerism/consumption, 8, 23–24, 34, 51–52, 96
consumption practices, 99–107

Conway, J., 8
Coole, D., 62
Cornell, D., 112–113
Council of Canadians, 6
Criddle, E., 9
Crossley, N., 114
cultural capital, 76–77
  subcultural capital, 94, 98, 99, 129, 134–136
cultural field, notion of, 15–16, 74–78, 88, 99, 121, 128
cultural phenomenon, 108
culture, role of state in, 47–48
Curtis, B., 36
Curtis, K., 141

data gathering methods, 142–155, 166–167nn1–3
Davies, I., 9
Day, R. J. F., 11
Dean, A., 161
democracy
  historicization of, 33–35
  liberal democracies, rights in, 30, 44–45, 56, 115–116, 164n6
DePass, C., 42, 164
dependency, genealogy of, 24–29, 30
detour, Ricoeurian, 34, 84, 142
Dewey, J., 41
Dillabough, J., 5, 10, 12, 45, 49, 60, 114, 143
DiMascio, A., 36, 162n1
distanciation, 34, 151
Dobbin, M., 6
dominant culture, 76
Dominion Institute, 38

economic recessions, 42–44
education. *See* citizenship education; public schooling
Edwards, F., 107
Emler, N., 26
emotional burdens, activist, 49–50, 59–63, 107
"ethical citizens," 44–45

ethnographic methodology, 142–152
European values, influence of, 7, 35–38, 84

family history, influence of, 73, 78–82, 89–90, 117–118, 135–136
Fanelli, C., 161
feeling, structures of, 21, 49, 63, 105, 109, 135
feminism/feminist theories, 16, 112–117, 129, 166n1
Fernández, C. M., 166
field of activism, 15–16, 74–78, 88, 99, 121, 128
Fine, M. L., 145
First Nations band, 64, 84
Foucault, M., 3, 19, 20, 21–22, 24–25, 47, 56
France, A., 10, 26
Fraser, N., 27–28, 112–113
Frazer, E., 26
"freedom of speech" protests, 66
Free the Children, 50
Free Trade Area of the Americas (FTAA), 1, 66, 69, 120
Frideres, J. S., 38
friendships, influence of, 123–125, 130
"Frosh week," 119–121
Fuller, S., 7
Furlong, A., 5

Gallagher, K., 154
Gauvreau, M., 27
gender
  activist engagement and, 59–63
  activist stereotypes and, 60, 62, 64, 66
  citizenship education and, 38–39
  neoliberal subjects and, 59–63
  women's voting rights, 38–39
genealogy of dependency, 24–29, 30
Give Us The Keys, 163

globalization, 4, 7, 41, 117
  antiglobalization, 11, 134, 155
Globe and Mail newspaper, 1
Goldstone, J. A., 11
"good citizen," notion of
  class exclusion and, 90–99
  cultural views of, 70–71
  historical views of, 33–35, 45–46
  police regulation of, 66–70
  societal notion of, 45–46, 50, 140–141, 163n5
  vs. notion of "bad activist," 3, 16, 50–53, 65, 123
  See also citizenship education
Gorard, S., 9
Gordon, H., 19, 24, 33
Gordon, L., 27
Gordon, T., 26
governance, youth citizenship and
  dependency, genealogy of, 24–29, 30–31
  overview, 19–21
  state role in, 19–25
governmentality theories, 8, 11
  Foucaultian, 3, 19, 20, 21–22, 24–25, 47, 56
  neoliberal governmentality, 21–24, 56
"government of individualization," 20–21
Graeber, D., 11
"Guantanamo North," 124
Guevara, C., 81
guilt, feelings of, 58–60, 63–64, 107, 138–139

Habermas, J., 71
habitus. *See* activist habitus
habitus shift, 116
Hall, S., 12, 47
Hall, T., 10
Hargrave, C., 6
Harper, D., 153
Harris, A., 10, 12, 60
Harris, M., 7, 165n7
Harris Conservatives, 7

INDEX 189

Heath, J., 81, 165–166, 165n9
Hebdige, D., 12
Hébert, Y., 9
Hernández, A., 71
heterosexual domination, 41
Highlander Folk School, 115–116
Highlander Research and
    Education Center, 116
Holland, J., 26
homosexuality, 41
human rights movements, 164n6
hunger strikes, 124

Ichilov, O., 44
icons, activist, 81
immigration, 41–45, 82–90
independence, youth, 25–29
individualism, neoliberalism and,
    8–9, 56–59
individualized consumerism, 8,
    23–24, 34, 51–52
individual responsibility, 45, 65–66,
    70–71, 140, 162–163n
"informed citizenship," 44–45
Institute for Public Policy Research,
    9, 44
"invited in," feeling of, 117–123,
    136–137
Ireland, 36–37

Jane magazine, 1, 60, 65
Jefferson, T., 12
Jones, R., 6, 9
Joshee, R., 35

Kach, N., 11, 97
Kahne, J., 54
Kahn-Harris, K., 13
Keil, R., 7
Kennelly, J., 5, 10, 12, 45, 131,
    140, 143, 163–164
Kershaw, P., 7
Kielburger, C., 50–53, 65, 71
King, M. L., Jr., 115
Kingston Immigration Holding
    Center, 124

Kirkness, V., 38
Klein, N., 166

Lahelma, E., 26
Langdridge, D., 145
language, authorized, 16, 99–101,
    115, 121, 129
Language and symbolic power
    (Bourdieu), 99
Lather, P., 144
law enforcement, 66–70
Lawler, S., 117
LeDuc, L., 9, 44
left-leaning politics, 54, 78, 80,
    127–128, 135, 164n2
Leighton, R., 9
Létourneau, J., 34
Levinson, B., 9, 44
Levitt, C., 82
liberalism, 65–66, 70, 107
    See also democracy;
        governmentality theories;
        neoliberalism
Lister, R., 60
London Feminist Salon Collective,
    113
Lousely, C., 93
Lovell, T., 112–115, 129, 136
Low, B. J., 41
Lucey, H., 49, 60, 62, 63, 178
Luttrell, W., 5

Macrae, S., 5
Maguire, M., 5
marches *vs.* protests, 70
Marcuse, H., 56
Marshall, T. H., 41
Martin, P. J., 13
martyrdom, 60
Mata, F., 42, 166
Mazurek, K., 42–44
McAdam, D., 11
McCarthy, J. D., 10
McDonald, K., 11, 97
McDonald's Corporation, 97
McGill University, 119

McGuinn, N., 9
McKay, L., 6
McLeod, J., 5, 114
McNay, L., 109, 112–113, 116–117, 129, 136
McRobbie, A., 2, 12
media, activist representations in, 1–3, 13–14, 48, 59–63, 70–71
Melody, J., 60, 62
Melucci, A., 10
mental hygiene movement, 41
Mercer, D., 107
"Me to We," 50
"middle-class performance," 77–83, 94–98, 109, 134–136, 140
minority groups. *See* multiculturalism; race
misrecognition, 76
Mitchell, K., 26, 45
Mizen, P., 27
Montreal, protests in, 67
Moore, R., 76
moral claims, 7, 8–14, 20, 39–40, 45–46
moral panics, influence of, 8–14
Mouffe, C., 71
multiculturalism, 43

National Association for the Advancement of Colored People (NAACP), 115–116
National Film Board of Canada, 41
nation-building, 36
neoliberalism
  citizenship education and, 25–26
  dependency and, 24–29, 30–31
  governmentality and youth, 21–24, 56
  individualism in, 8–9, 56–59
  political engagement, 56–59
  voting rights and, 56
neoliberal self-perfection, 24, 29, 51, 56, 97, 109, 139, 141–142
neoliberal subjectivity, 22, 24, 29, 34, 63

neoliberal subjects
  gendered subjects, 59–63
  policing of, 66–70
  state histories and cultural variations in, 63–66, 165n7
new social movement (NSM) theory, 10, 21
9/11 terrorist attacks, 66, 125
No One Is Illegal (NOII), 11
normalcy, cultural, 40–41, 84
NSM (new social movements), 10, 21

O'Malley, P., 22, 23
O'Neill, M., 9
Ong, A., 25
Ontario
  citizenship curriculum in, 44, 53
  conservative politics in, 7–8
  Ministry of Education, 52, 161n1
Ontario Coalition Against Poverty (OCAP), 11, 50–51, 120, 163n2
"oral education," 9
Ortner, S., 157–158
Osborne, K., 9
Osler, A., 9
Owens, T. J., 11

Palmer, B. D., 82
Pammett, J. H., 9, 44
Parks, R., 115–116
Parti Québecois, 7–8
Paulson, J., 161
"performing grunge," 77, 83, 90, 96–97, 109, 134–136
Perry, E. J., 11
Persson, D., 37
phenomenological methodology, 142–152
Phillips, A., 62
Piña, J. V., 166
placement, sense of, 75
policing, 66–70
Potter, A., 81, 165–166, 165n9

poverty. *See* antipoverty movements; class divisions/class exclusion
power relations, 19, 20, 21, 25–26, 134
practical knowledge, 75
Prentice, A., 36, 39–40
Progressive Conservatives, 8
progressive education, 41–44
protests
   anti-FTAA protests, 1, 66, 69, 120
   "freedom of speech" protests, 66
   in Montreal, 67
   in Quebec, 1, 8, 66, 69, 120
   in Toronto, 8
   vs. marches, 70
   See also social movements
Public Health Agency of Canada, 6
public institutions, 24
public schooling
   funding cuts to, 24
   inception of, 35–36, 162n1
   segregation in, 37

Quebec
   citizenship curriculum in, 44
   conservative politics in, 7–8
   nationalism/separatism in, 41
   protests in, 1, 8, 66, 69, 120
   social movements in, 11
Qureshi, S., 42, 164

"rabble-rousing" activism, 49, 66
race
   activist engagement and, 64–65, 66
   activist habitus and, 34, 71, 82–90
   activist identity and, 73
   citizenship education and, 34, 37–39, 41
   class divisions and, 82–84
   dominant culture and, 76
   education used for "civilizing," 38
   immigration and, 41–45, 82–90

   influence of history and, 130–131
   multiculturalism and, 43
Raco, M., 45
"radical," notion of, 77–78, 96, 98–99, 102, 134, 136
"Radical Frosh," 119–121
Reay, D., 49, 63, 114, 178
The rebel sell: why the culture can't be jammed (Heath and Potter), 165n9
reflexivity, 57, 140, 143–145, 149–150
relational agency, 17, 109, 112, 125–129, 131, 136, 139, 166n1
relationships
   influence on activist engagement, 123–125, 130
   as means of exclusion, 125–129, 130
   state and youth, 25–27, 30, 45–46, 49–50, 52–55, 164n6
research participants, methodology and, 152–155
resource mobilization (RM) theories, 10
responsibility, individual, 45, 65–66, 70–71, 140, 162–163n
Ricoeur, P., 15, 34, 113, 143–145, 151
rights of citizens, 44–45, 56, 115–116, 164n6
Robert, D., 7
Roberts, B., 12
Rodríguez, M. J., 166
Rose, N., 3, 17, 22–23, 29, 41, 45, 57, 102–103, 106
Ross, B., 41
Ryerson, E., 162n1

Sangster, J., 40
"save the world" ideals, 58, 60, 64
schooling. *See* citizenship education; public schooling
Scott-Bauman, A., 5
Seattle, social movements in, 11, 66

Seddon, A., 6
self-governing, 23
self-interest/self-development, 2, 20, 91
self-perfection, 24, 29, 51, 56, 97, 109, 139, 141–142
Semaganis, H., 37
September 11, 66, 125
Sewell, W. H., 11
Sewell, W. H., Jr., 114
Siltanen, J., 162
Skeggs, B., 74
Smith, L. T., 144
social change, activism and, 133–137
  political possibilities in modern age, 137–142
social exclusion. *See* class divisions/class exclusion; race
socialization, family history and, 79–80
social movements
  antipoverty movements, 11, 50–53, 120, 163n2
  civil rights movements, 115–116
  human rights movements, 164n6
  mental hygiene movement, 41
  moral panics, subcultures and, 8–14
  "new social movements," 21
  selfhood and identity within, 11
  types of, 10–11
social movement theories, 9–12
"social space," 75
social welfare, 24, 41–45, 162n3
socioeconomics. *See* class divisions/class exclusion
Sparks, H., 39
standardized exams, 42, 43
Stanley, T. J., 37, 38
Starkey, H., 9
Starr, A., 11
Stasiulis, D., 24, 161

state
  capitalism and, 27–29, 45, 47
  capitalist state, 27–29, 45, 47
  cultural role of, 47–48
  notion of, 21–24
  relationship with youth, 25–27, 30, 45–46, 49–50, 52–55, 164n6
  role of in governance, 19–25
state of exception, 164n6
"state-sanctioned mental categories," 16, 20, 65–66
Statistics Canada, 6
stereotypes, activist, 13–14, 48–49, 59–63, 66, 70–71
Strachan, J., 162n1
structures of feeling, 21, 49, 63, 105, 109, 135
Stryker, S., 11
subcultural capital, 94, 98, 99, 108, 129, 134–136
subcultures. *See* activist subcultures
subjectivity, neoliberal, 22, 24, 29, 34, 63
symbolic authorization, 13, 109
  authorized language, 16, 99–101, 115, 121, 129
symbolic economies, 74–78, 107

Tarrow, S., 10
Taylor, L., 4
Thornton, S., 76, 77, 98, 153
thoughtfulness, as quality, 29–30
Tilley, C., 10
Titley, B., 42–44
"tolerance," notion of, 24–25
Toronto
  conservative politics in, 7–8
  protests in, 8
Touraine, A., 10
Turner, D., 145

Valverde, M., 22, 23
Vancouver, conservative politics in, 7–8
vegetarianism, 102–103

Vidovich, L., 9
Viñuela, J. V., 166
voting rights
   neoliberal view of, 56
   for women, 38–39

Wacquant, L., 20, 33, 93, 138, 145, 149, 165, 166
Walkerdine, V., 60, 62, 63
Walsh, P., 36–37
Wang, E., 143
welfare dependency, 27–28, 162n3
welfare state, social, 41–42, 44–45, 162n3
Weller, S., 19, 26
Westheimer, J., 54
White, R. W., 11
Williams, R., 15, 47, 49, 144
Williamson, H., 10
Willis, P., 12, 20, 73, 143–146, 149, 151, 153
women
   "can-do" girls, 60
   feelings of guilt and, 58–60
   feminism/feminist theories, 16, 112–117, 129, 166n1
   voting rights of, 38–39
   "working-class performance," 77, 83, 94–98, 109, 134, 136

Yates, L., 5
Yates, M., 5, 9
Young, I. M., 71
Young, J., 5
Young, J. R., 43, 71
Young-Bruehl, E., 29, 106
Younnis, J., 5, 9
youth activism
   citizenship education and, 53–55
   class exclusion and, 78–82, 135
   emotional burdens and, 49–50, 59–63, 107
   engagement in, 50–55
   expansion of, 137–142
   family history, influence of, 73, 78–82, 89–90, 135–136
   family history and, 78–82, 117–118
   immigration and, 82–90
   implications for social change and, 133–137
   lack of by youth, 54–55, 66
   neoliberal subjects and, 56–59, 108, 134
   overview, 19–21
   pessimism about, 8–14, 33, 45, 54–55, 140
   policing and, 66–70
   political possibilities in modern age, 137–142
   relationships as resources for, 123–125
   for self-interest/self-development, 2, 20, 91
   societal perceptions of, 47–50
   stigma of activism, 48–49
youth activism, notion of, 133–137
youth activist identity
   autonomy and independence in, 25–29
   Canadian identity, ambivalence about, 84–87
   "change the world" ideals, 58, 60
   consumption practices and, 99–107
   feelings of guilt and, 58–60, 63–64, 107, 138–139
   feelings of inadequacy, 58–59
   finding balance in life, 60
   overview, 9–14, 140–142
   race and, 34, 73
   reactions to, 19–20
   state ordered categories of, 45
   thoughtfulness and ethical behavior, 29–30
   youth citizenship *vs.* legal status in, 25
   See also activist habitus
youth activists, perceptions of
   "bad activist" *vs.* "good citizen," 3, 16, 50–52, 65, 123
   class differences and, 64–65

youth activists, perceptions
    of—*Continued*
  controversy in, 65
  gender and, 64
  media representations, 1–3,
    13–14, 48, 59–63, 70–71
  public anxiety about, 66
  relationship with state, 25–27,
    30, 45–46, 49–50, 52–55,
    164n6
  societal representations of, 65–66
  stereotypes and labels of, 1,
    13–14, 48–49, 60, 65, 66,
    70–71
youth activist subcultures
  agency and, 111–112
  authorized language in, 13, 16,
    99–101, 115, 121, 129
  class divisions and, 90–99,
    107–109, 119
  "common culture" of, 20
  disciplining participants in,
    99–107
  dominant culture, 76
  internal power relations of, 97–98
  neoliberal subjects in, 56–59,
    108, 134
  overview, 11–14
  race and, 82–90
  "radical," notion of, 77–78, 96,
    98–99, 102, 134, 136
  shared values in, 99–107
  societal views about, 135
  subcultural capital, 94, 98, 99,
    108, 129, 134–136
  symbolic authorization, 109
  symbolic economy of, 74–78
youth "apathy," 55
youth citizenship
  constructing, 33–35
  dependency and, 24–29, 30–31
  expectations for, 25–26
  genealogy of dependency and,
    24–29, 30
  governance and, 19–25
  legal status *vs.* identity, 25
  opportunities for, 46, 161n1
  societal views about, 8–14
  See also "good citizen," notion of;
    youth activist identity
youth incarceration, 161n1

Zald, M., 10
Zizek, S., 107

The manufacturer's authorised representative in the EU is Springer Nature Customer Service Centre GmbH, Europaplatz 3, 69115 Heidelberg, Germany. If you have any concerns regarding our products, please contact ProductSafety@springernature.com

Printed and bound by CPI Group (UK) Ltd, Croydon, CR0 4YY

23/03/2026

02076673-0016